Sow What

Patrice Wallace-Moore

A TESTIMONY OF THE
POWER OF FAITH

ISBN:

CONTENTS

GIVE HONOR

(*Dedicated to whom Honor is due*)

In August of 2008, I was invited to speak for the annual Women's Day service at Blessed Hope Church in Albany, New York. The pastors, Ron and Barbara Howard (an anointed singer), had taken Albany by storm. The church was a former Catholic Cathedral they had converted into a thriving non-denominational church family.

Prior to every message preached over a *hosting pulpit,* there should be some preliminaries. On that day, here were my own:

Preliminary 1

There's not a friend like *The Lowly Jesus.* No, Not One; No, Not One. All praises belong to Him, and that is first and foremost.

Preliminary 2

When you are a visiting minister and not a pastor, you must give honor to the pastor who has opened their pulpit to you. Thus, I thanked the Howards for graciously opening their doors and sharing their pulpit. I am unsure if they knew then that their invitation would unleash a book in me. But many years later, I shared the vision with Pastor Barbara.

Preliminary 3

Next, I had to thank my pastor, who allowed me to preach under his watch and go to another church to minister. This show of honor and respect is necessary because some pastors do not permit their ministers to preach outside of their church. My pastor, the late Bishop Leon Dixon, was the pastor of The Emmanuel Pentecostal Faith Temple in Mount Vernon, NY. He was anointed to introduce and raise preachers, also some pastors, who preach the word of

God all around the world. He was a true visionary, a faithful Bishop. I will always love him as my Father in Ministry because he saw something in me that could have only come from God. He transitioned to his heavenly seat on *August 11th, 2018.*

Preliminary 4

Finally, I always have to thank my boyfriend of 41 years and my husband of 40 years, Lowes Moore, Jr., and my four children, Michelle, Shireyll, Lowes III, and Isaiah, for their love and patience. And, oh yes, as my children would say, "*Don't* forget Omar (our adopted son) and Jamayal (our godson who is now also our other adopted son.)"

When I began writing this book, my husband and I had only been married 26 years. Thus, this book is a thirteen-year testimony, the journey of faith and even more to get it published. I am now 40 years married and have two son-in-loves married to Michelle (Dakarai) and Shireyll (Steve), and a daughter-in-love married to Jamayal

(Angelica who we call Joi). They have given me and my husband four grandchildren, Amaya and Jade (Jamayal and Joi), Dakotah and Hartley (Dakarai and Michelle), and granddaughter Lanie (Steve and Shireyll).

INTRODUCTION

When I was asked to preach at Blessed Hope, the Lord immediately gave me a thought, but I needed to pray and ask for His guidance. He sent me to several scriptures, and I began to pray and ponder on what direction to take. Finally, the message came to me.

"So What?"

My first reaction was, "So what, what?"

God said to me, "So what! Now, work it!"

I laughed as I began to think about this journey. I remembered that my youngest daughter, Shireyll, used to know what to say to shake my foundation. I would say something to her. She would turn her head to the side, twist her lips, and say, "Whatever!" In other words, "So What!" I would shake in my inner being to keep from trying to shake the *so what* out of her. I remember thinking. *God, how could you possibly give me a message from two words that irritated me so much?* And then, it began to flow.

SCRIPTURES

I remembered Job and the scriptures where he received devastating news, *yet* he sinned not.

Job 1:14-22

14 *a messenger came to Job and said, "The*
oxen were plowing and the donkeys were
grazing nearby, 15 *and the Sabeans*
attacked and made off with them. They put
the servants to the sword, and I am the
only one who has escaped to tell you!"
16 *While he was still speaking, another*
messenger came and said, "The fire of God
fell from the heavens and burned up the
sheep and the servants, and I am the only
one who has escaped to tell you!" 17 *While*

he was still speaking, another messenger
came and said, "The Chaldeans formed
three raiding parties and swept down on
your camels and made off with them. They
put the servants to the sword, and I am the
only one who has escaped to tell you!"
18While he was still speaking, yet another
messenger came and said, "Your sons and
daughters were feasting and drinking
wine at the oldest brother's house, 19when
suddenly a mighty wind swept in from the
desert and struck the four corners of the
house. It collapsed on them and they are
dead, and I am the only one who has
escaped to tell you!" 20At this, Job got up
and tore his robe and shaved his head.
Then he fell to the ground in worship 21and
said: "Naked I came from my mother's
womb, and naked I will depart. The LORD
gave and the LORD has taken away; may
the name of the LORD be praised." 22In all
this, Job did not sin by charging God with
wrongdoing.

I also remembered the scripture where Paul

discussed ministry and the trials one must endure.

2 Corinthians 2:8–10

8We are troubled on every side, yet not
distressed; we are perplexed, but not in
despair; 9Persecuted, but not forsaken;
cast down, but not destroyed; 10Always
bearing about in the body the dying of the
Lord Jesus, that the life also of Jesus might
be made manifest in our body.

Then, I reflected on:

1 Corinthians 10:13

13No temptation has overtaken you except what is common to mankind. And God is faithful; he will not let you be tempted beyond what you can bear. But when you are tempted, he will also provide a way out so that you can endure it.

And:

2 Timothy 1:7

7 For God hath not given us the spirit of fear; but of power, and of love, and of a sound mind.

Although **2 Timothy 1:7** is the last scripture I reference in this section, I will mention others throughout this writing. Unless otherwise noted, *all Scriptures cited* are from the ***King James Version (KJV) of the Bible.***

CHAPTER 1

"NO BAD NEWS"

BAD NEWS

Many of us have endured some hardships and have been in situations where people bring us bad news. I remember watching *The Wiz*, the African American spin on *The Wizard of Oz*, which featured Michael Jackson as 'the Scarecrow' and Diana Ross as 'Dorothy.' At a critical point in the movie, Mable King, the "bad witch" sang the song "No Bad News." I am sure those who have seen this movie can hear her singing this song with all of her pizzazz. Yet, there is always a town crier in every community, church, or school. This person is the carrier of bad news. As a result, we often find ourselves expecting bad news. It seems people will respond accordingly when they hear it. They will either verbalize sympathy, "I feel bad for you;" empathy, "I've been there, and I understand what you're going through;" or apathy, "Oh well, get over it." When the bad news directly affects the person receiving it, the responses or reactions change. "What is going to happen to me? Oh my God! What am I going to do?"

Some people preface their comments by saying, "I have some good news and some bad news. Which would you like to hear first?" When that is said, feelings may come over you. I know that is true for me. I often feel neutralized because I know that whatever is good will be impacted by something terrible or that something wrong will be made better. How my day is progressing seems to dictate how I want the information to be served. If it's a good day, give me the bad news first, and I will overcome it with the good news. On a bad day, give me the good news first, and I will offset it with the blow of the bad news. Not just me, but many people receive both of these pieces of information and process them differently. It is like the adage, "the glass is half empty or half full." A positive mindset sees it as half full, and one who is negative (or some would say realistic) would see it as half empty.

In the book of **Job**, we find several episodes where Job receives terrible news. The first was when Job's oxen, donkeys, and servants perished. Before Job could take a moment to think about what happened, someone came to tell him that his sheep and servants had been killed. Once again, before he could take in all this, his servant informed him that marauders had captured and killed all his camels. Finally, the fourth servant came to tell him that the building that housed his children collapsed on them and killed them all. That had to be devastating. Not just one child, but all ten of his children died instantly. There was no good news in that. The Bible says Job handled all this without sinning or cursing God, even when his wife told him to. How did he do that? Each time Job received devastating news, only one person was left to report what had occurred. *Yet*, through all of this, Job sinned not. How did he do that? Or better yet, how did he *not*?

†

One day, early in my walk with Christ, I thought I had sent a money order to a bill collector. What I thought was the money order was returned in the mail a month later. What I had originally sent was the receipt for the money order and not the actual money order. So, where was the money portion? I didn't know, and I didn't have enough money to issue a new one. I didn't even realize what my options were. Right in my room, I had a tantrum and immediately began tossing things against the wall. One heavy item, my phone, hit the wall and fell to the floor. I then looked to the other side of my bed, where the phone lay on the floor, and I saw the money order sitting there (as if it had been looking at me the whole time). I was ashamed of my behavior, even though there was no one there to witness it. I felt ashamed before God. This mishap wasn't even a huge deal, and I fell. So, how on earth could Job lose everything and not sin? That amazed me, but it also put things into perspective for me. Job understood the principle of eternal versus temporal. He knew that God was the Giver and Taker, but in all this, God was still God.

Finally, the devil questioned God's protection of Job and was allowed by God to attack Job's physical body. Isn't that bad news in action? No one had to call him and tell him that. Instead, his friends and wife came by to rub salt into his wounds. His wife told him, "Curse God and die." His friends asked him, "What did you do wrong?" "Maybe you should repent and ask for forgiveness." None of the bad news deterred Job. He asked God, "Why?" He wanted to know what he had done to deserve such torture. He tried to defend himself against his friends and blamed God for his trouble. He did not understand what he was going through or why. Yet, throughout all this, he sinned not. In essence, he said, "So What!". It may not have presented that way based on his struggles and complaining, but he never cursed God.

God brought something to my attention. “So what” could be seen or perceived as ‘who cares’ or ‘whatever.’ When my daughter wanted to be sarcastic or talk back to me, she used to say, “Whatever!” Essentially, it was her way of saying she didn’t care what I was saying. I can’t mention here what I said in response. That remark could move anyone to anger. God changed my direction regarding this message. Instead of “So what?” God told me to change my topic to “Sow what?”

> By this point, Job had sowed good seeds. He prayed daily for his family. So, when the trials came, he could say, “Sow what?” He said, “Naked came I into out of my mother’s womb and naked will I return thither: the Lord gave, and the Lord hath taken away; blessed be the name of the Lord” (Job 1:21). However, once the troubles impacted his body, Job did not say, “So what? He lamented. He cursed the day he was born. Then, he wished he was dead or, better yet, had never been born. But he did not sin. He did not curse God.

Now that was his *sow what.*

I have stored up prayers. I have been faithful, and because of that, I knew I wouldn't waiver. At least, I thought I wouldn't. Reading the book of **Job** taught me to sow. In *due* season, he was able to reap because he didn't faint. The Bible declares that his latter became greater than his past, and God restored his losses far beyond anything he had before. God can do that for us, too! We must first understand how we process bad news, especially when it concerns us, our family, or people very close to us. But if I had *my* way, I would go back to the lyrics from that song in *The Wiz*, "No Bad News!"

CHAPTER 2

GOD HAS NOT GIVEN US A SPIRIT OF FEAR

What is it about bad news that moves us? Is it *fear*? Before we hear the news, we worry, anticipating what the news could be. In a moment, so many things flash through our minds. Did someone die? Will I die? Who is sick? Usually, our thoughts descend to the worse possible scenario. Consequently, this descent plagues us with fear.

What is *fear*? I have heard people say that fear is the opposite of faith or that fear occurs in the absence of faith. I actually believe fear is a precursor of faith. In other words, many of us who have great faith usually experienced something in our past that caused us to fear. Once we overcame that fear, faith set in.

When we feel unprepared for life's challenges, we can easily become more fearful of dying, consequently making us afraid of living. In 2010, my family and I experienced four deaths of loved ones close to us. The loss of my father, Lloyd P. Wallace, and my niece, Vonchelique Moore Liggins, impacted us the most.

My father had battled cancer for ten years. In the final months of his illness, we were unsure when he would expire, and it seemed like it was close on a few occasions. At night, I would sleep with my phone under my pillow, waiting for a call. I became paralyzed by the thought that he would pass away at night, and I would get the call notifying me that he was gone. I stopped my normal living, waiting for his life to end. I eventually gave up that fear and said, "Lord, if that is Your will, then so be it." But it wasn't easy. As the Lord would have it, my father died while surrounded by our immediate family. I held his right hand. My mother held his left hand. My brother rubbed his right shoulder. My sister rubbed his left shoulder. My husband was standing close behind me, and my brother-in-love was at my sister's back. I was not afraid at that moment.

However, earlier that week, I experienced an intense fear that I had never felt before. That night when I entered his room, I knew that my father had labored to breathe all day. I was sitting at his side, holding his hand. My husband and daughter were in the room with me. It was 11:30 on a Thursday night. Even though my husband and daughter were present, it felt like Dad and I were the only ones there. I held his right hand and placed my forehead in the bend of his elbow. Listening to his breathing was upsetting. Tears flowed steadily from my eyes. Shaken, I asked God to comfort him, but realizing his death could happen at any moment, I became anxious. More tears flowed, making my throat ache.

In his weakened state, my father looked into my eyes, and I could see my emotions moved him. He was determined to make sure this would not be the night. He then glanced over my head like something was behind me. I saw his eyes widen in fear, and his head began to shake side to side as if to say, "No! Not now!" I looked over my shoulder to the wall behind me, where my father seemed to be staring. All of a sudden, the cards that had been on the wall for some time began to fall, almost like they were popping off the bulletin board. My husband said, "Hey, what is going on here?" My heart raced. Instantly, I was terrified.

I now understand *why* in the Bible, an angel says, "Fear Not," when he appears. I felt the presence in the room with us and saw evidence of it at the bulletin board, where the cards were. When my father looked in the direction of the bulletin board and shook his head no, the presence (which I believe was an angel) left, knocking the cards off the bulletin board. I frantically called the nurse into the room to check on my dad. She said my father's blood pressure, heart rate, and oxygen level were normal. It was only then that the fear subsided. Why was I afraid? What didn't I understand? I am still not sure.

One thing I do know, my father did not die that evening. However, another member of his church did pass away around the same time the cards fell. To me, her death at that moment signified that the angel of death had left my dad with me and taken his fellow church member. She was the same woman my father told me he saw in his final days on this earth, and yet, they weren't even in the same hospital. Others may not believe this, but every time I think about it, it feels as real to me as the day I experienced it.

The following morning, my father's condition deteriorated. Doctors now listed him in critical condition. The hospital's chaplain came to him and administered Last Rites. All of the family came to say goodbye. Our immediate family, along with his siblings Joan, Ernie, Elaine, and some of his nieces, remained by his side. The social worker came and spoke with me and reminded me that many people die alone after the family leaves the room. She rekindled my fear that day. I struggled to leave the hospital that night. I did not want my father to die, and I'd get a call afterward. Instead, God granted us the ability to be together and see something I never thought I would.

His death happened right in front of my family and me. It was peaceful, and it was a blessing. It was a Saturday morning, July 31st, 2010. I was at a marriage retreat with my husband about 35 miles away from the hospital where my dad was. I woke up early and told my husband I would drive to the hospital to check on my dad. I was supposed to speak at 1:00 pm at the retreat. When I arrived at the hospital, I saw my brother seated beside my dad in his usual overnight spot. My brother never left my dad's side on the overnight shift for the entire duration of his hospitalization. My brother said, "Dad had a good night; he slept peacefully." When I looked at my dad's eyes, they were partially open, and his pupils did not move.

I said to my brother, "Dad is dying." He looked at me, befuddled and somewhat irritated. I called the nurse in from the nursing station and asked her to take my dad's blood pressure. The reading was 50/30. I immediately sprang into action. I called my mom, sister, and husband and told them to come immediately. My brother was upset that I called them, but I knew what was happening. I began to sing hymns to my dad and asked him to hang on until my mom came. When my mother arrived at 9:20 am, she immediately fell crying onto my dad's chest. My sister and brother-in-love (also Calvin) came in right behind her. Not long after, around 9:45 am, my husband arrived. We all stood there in tears, watching Dad's labored breaths get slower and slower. At 9:50 am, I led my family in a heartfelt prayer to release my dad. I finished my prayer at 10:00 am with these words. "Father, into Your hands I commit his spirit, In Jesus' name." Just as I finished my prayer and said, "Amen," my father took his last breath.

My brother looked at me and asked, "How did you do that?"

I said, "What?"

He said, "Know that Dad would die like that?"

I said, "I didn't do anything; God did it?"

The fear was gone, and my faith flourished. God allowed me to face it. It is not something I want to become familiar with, but I am not afraid of death, and thus, I am not afraid to live. I now understand the scripture that says, "God has not given us a spirit of fear but of love, power, and a sound mind." Thank you, Lord, and thank you, Daddy!

What experiences have you had when you felt the

most fear? How did you handle that?

CHAPTER 3

IN DESPAIR

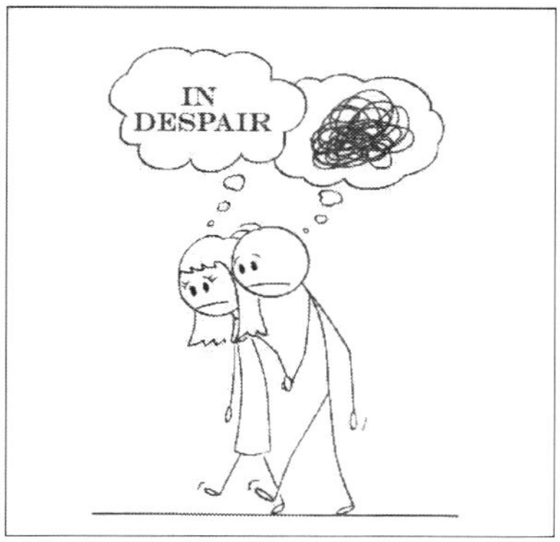

2 Corinthians 2:8–10

*8We are troubled on every side, yet not
distressed; we are perplexed, but not in
despair; 9Persecuted, but not forsaken;
cast down, but not destroyed; 10Always
bearing about in the body the dying of
the Lord Jesus, that the life also of Jesus
might be made manifest in our body.*

I struggled with the concept of despair. I don't even like saying the word because it puts heaviness in my belly. As a Godly woman, I am almost embarrassed to say, “At times, I have been in utter despair.” But really, what is despair?

According to the online version of Merriam-Webster’s dictionary, **despair** means to lose all hope or confidence. Wow! I have really been in that place before. The funny thing is, some Christians made me feel like I wasn’t really saved because I was in such inward pain. They would say something like:

“Where is your faith?”

“Lift your hands and praise God anyway!”

“Stop crying. The people need to see you strong in your *go through*.”

I want to let you know that if you really believe in God yet have moments when you have felt great despair, you don’t automatically lose your Christian card. So, to all those who have made it to the point where you never felt this way, congratulations! I hope you *never* feel this paralyzing emotion! To the rest of us who have been there and done that, I am sure you can still clearly remember a moment you felt that pain, and you want to move on from that memory quickly.

†

Years later, I was asked to lead a song that was originally recorded by Meaghan Williams entitled "I Made It." The song begins with lyrics based on the **Isaiah 54:17** scripture, "No weapon formed against me shall prosper." It then takes on a rapid call and response where, line for line, I would declare victory, and the choir would repeat after me in robust harmonies. Victory declared.

For Christians, however, **despair** as we understand it means to *lose all hope of winning or to lose heart.* That song immediately jumped into my head. My feet started tapping, and my head swayed back and forth, yet no music played outwardly. Isn't it amazing when you can play encouraging songs in your head amidst adversity? I had to learn to keep that song in my encouragement bank.

†

I truly wish I had heard that song ringing in my head when my son Isaiah was born with Spina

Bifida or three years later when doctors gave my oldest son a grim diagnosis and told us the condition would lead to his death at an early age, in his twenties or thirties. I couldn't figure out how my God, who was so awesome to me, would bring me to such levels of pain and tears. *How could this happen to me? I prayed, praised, worshipped, served, and worked with the best of the saints. "So, why was God picking on me? Why was this hurting so much?"*

A little backstory about my boys may clarify why I felt as I did.

By 1991, we had two beautiful daughters. My husband and I were doting parents, but I wasn't satisfied; I wanted and prayed for a son. The following year, we had our first son, born two hours before his dad's 35th birthday. He was the prince. He was the first grandson born after eight granddaughters, carrying his father's and grandfather's name. He was truly spoiled. More about him later.

Three years later, our second son was born. His birth was difficult, as he was born with spina bifida and taken immediately from us and brought to the major medical center in another town.

Spina bifida is a birth defect where there is incomplete closing of the backbone and membranes around the spinal cord. There are three main types: spina bifida occulta, meningocele, and myelomeningocele. The most common location affected is the lower back, but in rare cases, it may be the middle back or neck. Occulta has no or only mild signs, which may include a hairy patch, dimple, dark spot, or swelling on the back at the site of the gap in the spine. Meningocele typically causes mild complications with a sac of fluid present at the gap in the spine. Myelomeningocele, also known as open spina bifida, is the most severe form. Associated problems include poor ability to walk, problems with bladder or bowel control, hydrocephalus, a tethered spinal cord, and a latex allergy. (https://en.wikipedia.org/wiki/Spina_bifida)

Isaiah had myelomeningocele *spina bifida.* Doctors told us he would never walk and gave us a whole list of other things we should and should not ever expect him to be able to do. The tears that came were countless. This diagnosis rattled us and shook our faith. I remember the first time my husband and I visited him at the Westchester Medical Center Neonatal Intensive Care Unit. We were able to bring his older siblings. Isaiah was so tiny and looked so helpless.

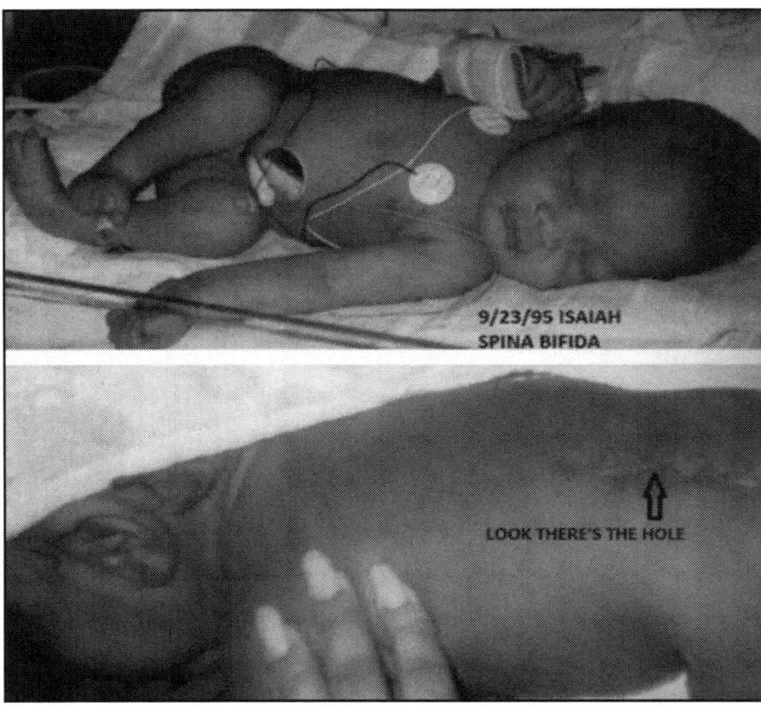

Although my heart was trembling, the kids brought that same level of faith I had as a nine-year-old when my little sister had a life-threatening illness. As we were all looking at him in his little incubator, a nurse approached and said, “Do your kids know your son is special?”

“Special,” I said to myself. Being quick-witted, I responded, “Yes my kids know my son is special because they are *all* special, and we are a special family!” The nurse turned around on her heels and walked away.

I felt insulted. Inside, I wanted to be angry. But big brother Lowesie came to the rescue. He looked in the incubator, and with his three-year-old high-pitched voice and deep dimples, he said, “Mommy, I am going to teach Isaiah to walk, and I am going to teach Isaiah to talk.” Then, he spread his arms as wide as he could and yelled, “I am going to teach Isaiah how to love everybody!” For a moment, that little boy encouraged me to know how truly special we are.

Later that day, they isolated our son, fearing he had a contagious disease (which he did not). My parents took my children home after their one-hour visit. That evening when my husband

and I left the hospital, I remember getting in the car and feeling despair engulf me like a tsunami. I was leaving my tiny, helpless baby there in the hands of strangers. I had just had him the day before. During those first hours postpartum, my emotions were all over the place. Soon, I began to sob loudly as my husband somehow drove us home. We didn't speak. We couldn't say anything at all. We reached the exit nearest my parents' house, and suddenly, he pulled over. Then, I heard the loudest cry from him I had ever heard, even though he had cried when his grandfather passed away twelve years earlier. By the time we walked into my parents' house, we had swollen faces with red noses and bright red eyes. Our fragile emotions caused my parents to cry, as well. But together, we all held each other until our strength came. Our kids really didn't understand, or so we thought. But they experienced that time with us. My kids are very special *and* absolutely amazing.

Days after he was born, Isaiah had to undergo his first surgery to place his spinal cord inside his spinal column. I remember rushing to the hospital the morning of the surgery to give him a kiss before they prepped him. But when I got there, he was already in surgery. I went crazy, yelling for my baby. How dare they take him without me seeing him first? To me, he was so helpless inside the Neonatal Intensive Care Unit (NICU). He needed his mommy. His mommy needed him, too. I was overcome with despair once again.

A few days after his first surgery, they finally let me hold him and nurse him. I was bonding with my baby. Everything looked like it was going well. The doctor said there was one more hurdle we would have to jump, and we needed to watch and wait for a few days. There was a disorder called Chiari Malformation Type II. It affects many Spina Bifida babies and is evident by fluid building on the brain or hydrocephaly. The doctor told me Isaiah was doing well and that he would be able to come home. He didn't think he had the malformation. I sighed, having a moment of relief. But it was brief.

Just as we thought we could bring him home, the test results revealed there *was* fluid increasing on his brain. Isaiah would need to have surgery. My husband was out of town. I was alone at the hospital and had just finished nursing him when I was approached by a neurosurgery resident. Isaiah was going to need a ventriculoperitoneal (VP) shunt inserted into his brain to drain the fluid from his brain into his stomach. During the discussion, another resident came to me and asked me to fill out Advanced Directives or Do Not Resuscitate (DNR) forms in case there was a problem during surgery.

As I read the forms, I began to sob. The fear that came over me was so overwhelming I could barely breathe. *What am I doing signing this form? Of course, I want my baby resuscitated.* But I signed the DNR anyway. When I look back on that day, I don't know why I did that. This was true despair. After I signed the papers, I went back into the NICU and kissed my baby boy Isaiah, wondering if I'd ever see him alive again. I went to the parking lot and sobbed uncontrollably. I blamed myself for his illness. I felt I was being punished. Even as I write these words, I am sobbing like it was yesterday.

†

Why Was I Being Punished?

I had already had three children and didn't want a fourth. For the first few months of my pregnancy, I tried to pretend I wasn't pregnant. My career was taking off, and I wanted to go back to school to get my PhD. I had started making appearances on the Montel Williams Show, and I had learned to manage three children with ease. A fourth was just going to mess things up for me. So, I felt I was being punished because I didn't want God's gift for my life. Little did I know how much this experience would define and strengthen my faith. Little did I know God saved the best for last!

That night, after speaking with the resident, I drove home in tears. Sobbing, I called my family from my cell phone to tell them what the doctor had said. I was scared. Isaiah's godmother, Marion, had my girls at her Hair Salon. She brought them home to me, but I couldn't stop crying. The girls were upset because they saw their mommy devastated. So, Marion took them and my oldest son to my parents' home. My husband was away for the weekend. Marion decided to stay overnight with me, so we could go to the hospital together the next morning. I prayed and cried most of the night. I only fell asleep after sheer exhaustion had taken over.

The next morning, I woke up before sunrise. Reverend Paul Morton (Greater St. Stephen Church—New Orleans, LA.) was on television preaching about faith. I held onto his every word and gained the strength to get up out of my bed of exhaustion and despair. Marion and I arrived at the hospital before the nurses even had Isaiah prepped. That was important to me because the last time he had surgery, they had taken him to the Operating Room before I even made it to the hospital. Marion, an ordained minister, prayed for Isaiah, and in her very compassionate way, she prayed for all the babies in the NICU. The medical team came and prepped him for surgery. We went downstairs, and within twenty minutes, the doctor came and told us the surgery was over, and all went well. I praised God that very moment. Tears of desperation turned to tears of joy. Despair had been defeated. *That was ROUND 1.*

Isaiah would undergo three more surgeries before the age of five (including a repair of his shunt and brain surgery). However, there was no longer a sense of despair. We had already experienced God's mercy and grace, so we expected it. *Then came ROUND 2.*

†

ROUND 2.

Our oldest son, Lowes III (Lowesie), was quite precocious. He walked, talked, and did everything relatively early. He was spoiled, though. He had the greatest dimples and smile and charmed everyone with whom he came in contact. There was great expectation over his life. He was born to two successful athletes who had both excelled in their careers. We expected nothing less for his future.

At age four, he ran track with the Boys and Girls Club track team, where my husband was the Executive Director. At the time, he was winning every track event for the four-year-old group. Just before he turned five, we put him back on the team. This time, he couldn't finish *any* race. He could barely run 30 yards. He would fall at school and couldn't walk without being escorted. He also couldn't hold anything in his fingers without dropping it. His hands shook, and he shuffled his feet like someone with Parkinson's Disease. My husband and I began contacting doctors about the changes we noticed in him. At first, they thought we were overreacting, but the situation worsened. By the time we got him to a neurologist, they had to conduct a muscle reflexology test. They diagnosed him with polyneuropathy (weakened or dead nerves impacted his muscles). The initial diagnosis was some form of Muscular Dystrophy.

The worst thing they could do was give me a diagnosis. I went straight to my computer to review the symptoms of Muscular Dystrophy. The list read as follows:

- *Frequent falls*
- *Difficulty getting up from a lying or sitting*

position
- *Trouble running and jumping*
- *Waddling gait*
- *Large calf muscles*
- *Learning disabilities*

Lowesie had the first four of the six symptoms listed above. Again, fear and desperation flooded my faith. I asked God, "Why? Really? This is the son I prayed for. The one I planned."

He was my perfect little boy. I already had one child I would have to protect for the rest of my life. I had to regain my composure. "Duchene Muscular Dystrophy" is a recessive *X-linked* gene that would result in eventual paralysis and death. *X-linked* also meant it would have to come from me or my side of the family. *Why my side?* That's because all men have one X chromosome and one Y chromosome. All women have two X chromosomes. So, if the disease had come from my husband's X chromosome, my husband would also have the condition. Since my son was a male, he could not have gotten an X-linked gene from my husband. My husband had given him his Y chromosome. This disease had to have come from me. To determine if it came from me, the doctor ordered genetic testing. I felt the weight of the world on my shoulders, waiting for those results. Then, that day came. Inhale. Exhale. The results of the tests were negative. Thank God! Despair and fear lifted, but only for a moment.

The symptoms did not dissipate. Lowesie was still falling; he was weak; he had poor muscle tone, etc. We had to find out what was wrong. After further testing, the doctor called us in to discuss a diagnosis. It was a Wednesday afternoon. I brought my video camera to see what exercises Lowesie would need to learn that week. The doctor brought us into the room. He looked down before he saw that I was waiting to make eye contact. He said, "We believe your son has a disorder called Charcot Marie Tooth."

"What?" I had never heard of that before.

He went on to say it was an autoimmune disease. Also, in this case, it was *X-linked.* Again, that means it would have had to come from me or my side of the family. He said it would eventually lead to paralysis. There was no cure. Life expectancy was only up to his 20s or, at best early 30s.

At that very moment, I disappeared. I felt like

I was above the room, looking down at the doctor discussing his condition with me. It was like an out-of-body experience. His words sounded like the teacher in the Charlie Brown TV show, "Wah, wah, wah-wah." I couldn't bear to listen to any more bad news. I didn't remember anything else except floating to the car. Lowesie held our hands as we walked, and he could see the tears streaming down my face. "What's wrong, Mommy," he said in his usually high-pitched voice. I couldn't even speak. When I stepped out of the car to go into my parents' home, I realized I left the camera at the doctor's office. I frantically began looking for the camera. The whole time I had the camera with me, and because I had gone into a deep fog, I had no memory of picking up the camera.

When I walked into my house, I immediately

called Marion. She had been with me through Isaiah's ordeal. I trusted her. I tried to tell her what was wrong, but with every breath, the tears and sobbing choked out my words. She finally just told me to hold on, "shut up," and she began a prayer of faith through the phone. It felt like her prayer became arms that wrapped around me to comfort me during this time. Her words strengthened me enough to go to choir rehearsal. Yes, I said choir rehearsal. I had just received devastating news about my son, but I had to remain faithful to my Godly assignment.

I was the choir director. It was Wednesday night. I was teaching songs for a concert we had scheduled for Sunday. I went over every song but never told anyone what was happening with me. Rehearsal usually ended faithfully at 9:00 p.m. The choir members began putting on their coats at 8:58 p.m. I began to pray, and while praying, I finally released what I had been holding in for the whole rehearsal. Listening to those songs minister to me required a lot of strength because I knew the women wanted to leave at nine. While praying, something came over me. I went to the altar and knelt. I cried out to God in despair to help my son. I still never told the choir what was going on. I stayed on the altar until 11:00 p.m. No one left. They prayed with me. When I got up, I began to think about the *X-linked* CMT. I went through my maternal family history as far back as my mother, and I could go. We couldn't find that illness or anything like it anywhere. It just couldn't be!

God's Answer

The next day I was at work. I don't remember if I told anyone what was happening. I was still in a fog. All day I kept thinking about my family history. Around 4:00 p.m., my husband called me and loudly said, "Trice, the doctor called, and they need to see us tomorrow. He thinks there is a mistake in the diagnosis."

I jumped out of my seat and yelled, "Mistake,

no! God, yes!" I began to praise God for His excellent work. I had already believed God had answered my prayers. He did it before, and He would and will do it again.

The next day we took Lowesie to the hospital for tests. It was a long day, but they had to give him a spinal tap to look for a virus. Yet, they found no virus. They discovered antibodies had unleashed to fight a virus that wasn't there. So, the antibodies attacked his spinal cord and the protective sheath around it. That impacted his peripheral nerves, which led to weakness in his hands, fingers, feet, and toes. It replicated and looked like the symptoms of Muscular Dystrophy and Parkinson's. He was now diagnosed with Chronic Inflammatory Demyelinating Polyneuropathy (CIDP). Although the name sounds intimidating, the prognosis was the best of the previous two. The bottom line, it was treatable and curable. He received a mega dose of immunoglobulin that day and four consecutive days of intravenous immunoglobulin treatment. This treatment was similar to that used for people who have had Leukemia. Immediately, Lowesie regained much of his strength.

Later that year, he returned to track. His first race was the 50-yard dash. I waited for him at the finish line, yelling his name and waving my hands frantically. He came in last place, but I was there. I picked him up, swung him around, and cheered like he had won. I am sure it confused many, but as small as he was, Lowesie understood what was happening.

When I returned to the bleachers, a little kid said to me, "Why are you so happy? He lost! He came in last place." He looked at his parent and started to laugh.

I said, "You have no idea what we've been through. The most important thing is that Lowesie finished. He finished." I cried as I held on to my miracle son that day.

Despair was defeated in ROUND 2.

†

Today, Lowesie is a college graduate and an accomplished singer who is pursuing a career in acting. Since he couldn't continue his athletics immediately after his experience, what he did do was begin to sing in church. His first song was "According to Your Way." God did things according to His way.

Have you ever felt despair? What did it do to you and how did you get past it?

CHAPTER 4

I SURRENDER ALL

I have faced so much adversity that I often wondered how I made it through. When I look and see reminders of some of the challenges others have faced, I am embarrassed that I even made a fuss. Understanding that, going through my *go through,* felt like the worst experience ever. Each event had brought me to my knees. Each event consequently stripped me of all of my so-called pride. Each humbled me and brought me to the place of surrender.

What comes to mind when you read or hear 'surrender'? Do you think the person who surrenders is weak? Do you think the person is

defeated? Have you ever surrendered to anything? Why is surrendering even mentioned?

†

I preached a sermon once that said, "I am surrounded, but I won't surrender." Although I delivered that message with great excitement, what the audience did not understand, and I am sure I did not clarify, was that I had surrendered. But it was to whom I surrendered that mattered. I surrendered to Jesus. I gave all I had in me to Him. And when I did, He lifted my burdens. That couldn't happen until I let go, until I gave up, until I surrendered, casting my cares upon Him.

Surrendering to God is not a sign of weakness. Surrendering to God is a sign of strength. The Bible says in **2 Corinthians: 12:9,** "And He said unto me, My grace is sufficient for thee: for my strength is made perfect in weakness." In other words, when I am at my weakest, I have to rely on Christ. But I first must acknowledge and accept my weakness.

What is weak? Not my faith. But my heart and my flesh get weak. I am human, and if you are reading this book, so are you. I am sure you have had times in your life when you felt that you didn't have control over a situation, and the outcome had nothing to do with you but everything to do with the will of the Lord. It was at that time that all you could do was relinquish your will to His will. That is how I felt when dealing first with my son Lowes, then my son Isaiah, then my dad, and definitely, my mom.

Recently, I have been given a diagnosis that makes me feel as if I am next on that journey. But I am preemptively surrendering to the Lord ahead of time because I know He will give me the strength to make it through.

According to *Merriam-Webster's online dictionary,* the definition of **surrender** is 'to yield to power or to give up completely.'

There were times I had to deliver over my feelings and fears to my Higher Authority. Desperation led to my surrendering. It was when I became my most desperate and when I felt I could no longer expend another ounce of my fleshly energy that I surrendered.

Years ago, there was a movie in theaters entitled, *An Officer and a Gentleman.* In this movie, the main character, Zack Mayo, is a man who does not have compassion for others. He is selfish and arrogant, and he only cares about himself. At least, that is how he presents himself on the outside. The drill sergeant, who is in charge, is tasked with breaking the will of this soldier. He does so by making Zack work harder than everyone else and by fighting him and trying to make him quit, surrender, or give up. The sergeant ultimately won that battle but in a different way. The soldier did give up; he did surrender. He surrendered his will, his arrogance, and his selfishness. In the most poignant scene, Zack is in a battle of wills with the drill sergeant. The drill sergeant punishes Zack to drive him to quit. Then, he antagonizes Zack even further to make him quit. Finally, when Zack is physically and emotionally exhausted and has reached his limit, Zack cries out, "I got no place to go!" It is at that point that he surrenders the truth. He set himself free.

During my experiences, God had to reshape my will and my arrogance. Although I didn't think I was arrogant, looking back, I know I was. God undressed me and humbled me. He put on new garments. He taught me how to surrender my will to Him early on and to trust Him.

> Jesus did just that when He was in the garden of Gethsemane praying, and He looked to His Father and asked Him to remove the cup from Him that He was about to drink. His silent Father didn't have to answer. Jesus said, "Father nevertheless not my will but THY WILL

be done." In His statement, Jesus was surrendering to His Father's will. Moments later, when the soldiers came to arrest Him, Peter attacked one of the soldiers with a sword, slicing off his ear. Jesus replaced the ear, healing the soldier. And although He had the power to resist, Jesus surrendered and scolded Peter. Jesus then gave Peter this powerful Word of advice: *If you live by the sword, you will die by the sword.*

Lastly, on the cross, just after He uttered a few words that live on annually and worldwide in the *Seven Last Sayings*, the Bible says Jesus surrendered (gave up) the ghost. None of these instances were a sign of weakness. You fight along with the Lord until victory is in your hands. The enemy seeks to kill, steal, and destroy. He wants you to give up to him. But, when God is on your side, there is no surrender to the enemy.

Moses told the Israelites in **Deuteronomy 31,** when they were about to cross over the Jordan River into the promised land of Canaan that he would not be able to go over with them. He told

Joshua and Caleb not to be afraid because the Lord would go before them. He told them not to give up. But they had to surrender their fears and replace fear with courage and faith. No matter what you are facing today, I encourage you to surrender your fear, surrender your thoughts, surrender negative words, and turn them all over to Jesus.... In **1 Peter 5:7,** we are told to, "cast our cares upon Him because He cares for us."

Today, I cast away my fears. Whatever Your will Lord, I will obey. What have you surrendered to God? Looking deep inside what are you holding on to that you know needs to be surrendered to God?

CHAPTER 5

PRAYER CHANGES THINGS

I learned how to pray at a very young age. I remember the first time God answered a prayer of mine. It was the most powerful experience of my life. As a young child, I learned the cliché prayers such as:

Now I lay me down to sleep.
I pray the Lord my soul to keep.
If I should die before I wake,
I pray the Lord my soul to take.

I don't know how you feel about that prayer, but as a child, it sure made me think. *If I should die before I wake? Huh!* So, falling asleep wasn't easy for me. I used to get up in the middle of the night in fear of what could cause me to die. *Fire? Yep, a fire could kill me.*

As a kid, I saw two big fires, and I knew fire could cause death. Both fires created explosions. One was a stove, and the other was a car. Well, that was enough for me. *If I should die before I wake?* .... Well, if I don't go to sleep, then that won't happen. I had heard if the building we lived in caught fire, the lights would go out. So, I would wait until my parents went to sleep, and I would go into the hallway by the front door, place my head on the floor, and look beneath the apartment door to see the light in the hallway. Surely, if the light went out there, that would mean FIRE. I would be able to get up and run to save everybody. Well, that is where my dad would find me and put me back to bed. But the fear remained. I guess that is why I am saved today because I am afraid of fire.

The next prayer I learned:

God is great.
God is good.
Lord, I thank you

For our food.
By His hand we must be fed.
Give us, Lord, our daily bread.

This prayer meant we could eat. As a child, this prayer didn't last long, and we were glad about that. As we get older, some of these meal prayers last so long; the food gets cold. But it is important to teach our children to pray, even if it is repetitive.

What prayers did you say?

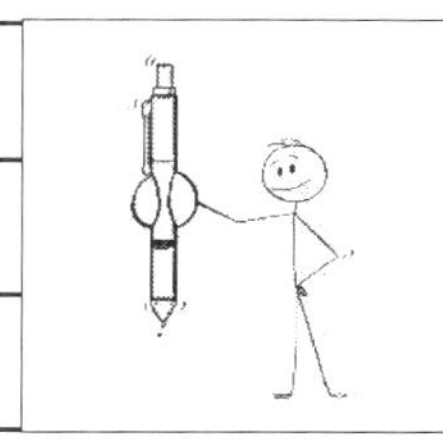

Last but not least, we learned *The Lord's Prayer*. This one was long. I don't quite remember when I learned it. I just know, at some point, I knew it. I love how this prayer provides a framework for all prayers and can be found in **Matthew 6:9b-13**.

9b Our Father which art in heaven, hallowed be Thy name.
10 Thy kingdom come, Thy will be done on earth, as it is in heaven.
11 Give us this day our daily bread.
12 And forgive us our debts, as we forgive our debtors.
13 And lead us not into temptation, but deliver us from evil: For Thine is the kingdom, and the power, and the glory, forever. Amen.

This prayer teaches us to reverence God and His power before we ask anything of Him. Plus, it attributes to Him all that belongs to Him (*kingdom*, *power*, and *glory*). I didn't even have a clue about that when I first heard this prayer. Honestly, I think I learned that as a teenager or even young adult.

†

The first time I prayed a *real* prayer—a prayer that had meaning—it was the prayer of a child who had nothing but true hope and desire. That happened when I was eleven years old, and wow, I remember it like it was yesterday. It was around 1974 or 1975 when we had just been in our new home in Mount Vernon, NY, for a little over a year. Everything seemed to be going well. My parents got a real Christmas tree, and the house smelled like pine. Gifts were everywhere. Everything seemed normal. Note the operative word here, *seemed.* Little did we know, my little sister Dierdre (Dede) was getting sick. By mid-week, she had a fever, and spots were on her face. When my frantic mom brought her to the doctor, the doctor saw her, quarantined her, and told my mom she had measles or something and she had to take her home immediately. My mom was upset but obedient.

By the time New Year's Eve came, Dede was getting worse. She had diarrhea. Blisters were on her lips and in her mouth. Her fingernails were coming off. Her eye sockets were bleeding. She looked like a monster. The name of this disease—we found out later—was Steven Johnson's syndrome. My cousin's name is Steven Johnson, but the disease was not named after him.

That New Year's Eve, it snowed like crazy. There had to be at least a foot of snow on the ground. That didn't keep my parents from their partying. The house was filled with guests. People were drinking, and all sorts of stuff went on. I was paying attention to Dede. Something was wrong with my little sister. The one who, when my mommy brought her home as a baby, I wanted her to be *my* baby. The one, who was such a brat; she would embarrass me when our mom would drop me off at elementary school, because she wanted to stay with me. Yep, she was a pain, but she was my pain. I didn't want to see her hurting, but I could not help her. I was *so* scared.

My dad's friend, Joe, and his wife, Shirlee, were there. Shirlee was a nurse. She took one look at Dede, took her temperature, and told my mom to take her to the hospital immediately. She was very stern. My dad said, "No." He thought driving in that major snow storm was too dangerous. Dad and Uncle Joe got into a big argument over this, and Uncle Joe won. He, Aunt Shirlee, and my mom wrapped Dede in blankets and took her to

Westchester Medical Center. Even as I think about this, I get teary-eyed, for their actions at that moment saved her life. They admitted Dede into the Children's ward as soon as they reached the hospital.

The next morning, the phone rang early. I got up and noticed Dede was no longer in bed with me. I panicked and ran downstairs and saw my dad talking on the phone. Then, he let out a horrible sound of despair and fell to his knees. He put his head in his hands and sobbed. I had never seen my dad so distraught. I immediately thought my baby sister had died. I ran upstairs, barely touching steps. I went into my room, threw all of my trophies on the floor, and destroyed my room. I told God I hated Him for letting my sister die. I just kept yelling, "I hate you! I hate you!"

My mother's brother had stayed over, and he came upstairs and saw me cursing God, and he slapped me in my face. When I came to, I looked at him. He asked me why I was doing that. I said, "God let my sister die."

He said the most powerful words I could have heard, "She is not dead. The doctor said she might die. She might end up blind or brain damaged."

I was stunned. Why was my dad crying so hard? She's not dead. Then, I realized what I had done. I fell to my knees and yelled, "God, I am sorry! Thank you for not letting her die. Please let her live. I promise I will never yell at her again. I will never hit her again. I will never fight her again. Please, God. Amen." That is probably the most earnest, heartfelt prayer I had ever made up until that point and is still the most powerful to me today.

Dede stayed in the hospital for weeks. She made a tape recording at one point, stating she didn't know if she would live or die. My parents played it for my brother and me. I bawled. One day my best friend Lisa's mom took me to hear Rev. Dr. Wyatt T. Walker preach. They had a prayer line, and I got on it. When I got to the front, they asked me why I was there. I said in my little voice, "My baby sister is sick, and I want her to live." They prayed for her.

It wasn't long after that day that my sister was due to come home. She had received so many toys that my family had to carry multiple bags into our home, like luggage. One of the toys dropped as they entered the house, and Dede told me to put it down because it was her toy. She was only nine, doing what nine-year-olds do. But I was eleven, and I had not really seen my parents for weeks because they were with her. *And now, she wanted to be mean?* So, I unleashed a barrage of threats and harsh words. They came out so fast that I didn't even realize what I was saying. I knew I was in trouble. I was jacked up by everyone in that house that day.

My mom's dad was there, and he was a majestic man. He was good-looking, smart, and a principal. He grabbed me and lectured me for two hours. By the time he finished, I was like: *Just beat me.* I never understood the power of that moment until I became an adult.

Seven years later, I was about to be baptized, and I remembered that I had made a promise in my prayer to God. I said I would never yell at my sister, hit her, or fight her. Well, I had gone back on my promise on numerous occasions, BUT GOD...

God kept His promise. So, that day, I totally surrendered my life to Him. I accepted Him as my personal Lord and Savior. That day, my life was *never* the same again. Prayer changed my life, and I have been praying ever since.

I challenge you to try prayer and, like in the movie *War Room,* write down your answered prayers. You *will* be amazed. I sure am!

I've shared this prayer experience I had as a child with many friends. One of my friends and I discussed how genuine children's prayers are. That prompted me to remember my daughter, Michelle. When she was nine years old, one of the ministers in our church got sick. She was so ill that the doctors thought she would die. Several of us decided to go to the hospital to visit her one day. That same day, our church called a fast with the intention of also praying for her healing. Michelle was in either the fourth or fifth grade at the time. When she got to school, she told her teacher she had to fast and pray for a minister at church. The teacher was stunned and yet, in awe of this little child. When lunchtime came, the teacher asked Michelle if she wanted to go to lunch. Michelle told her, "No." She wanted to stay in class and pray. The teacher decided to stay with her and told her if she got hungry, she could eat the apple the teacher had sitting on the desk. Michelle put her head down and prayed. Nine years old, she knew what to do.

I have no idea what she prayed. But I do know this. Later that evening, I and several others in ministry visited Sister Vera. The staff told us she might not make it through the evening. She looked so bad. When we went into her room, we walked past her to the other patient. Then, we heard her feeble voice call to us. I was blown away by the decline in her condition. I went over to her, hugged her, and whispered in her ear that Michelle had fasted and prayed for her.

Immediately, she lifted her hands and spoke in her heavenly language. She began to speak encouraging words, and her voice was no longer feeble. It was powerful and convincing. Those of us in the room left so encouraged that when we got outside, we stood in the hospital's parking lot in awe and talked for over an hour about the goodness of God. Sister Vera was healed and made whole. She eventually became an Elder in our church with many more stories to tell. Her healing came from fasting and praying. A child's prayer was heard that day. Today, that child is an adult who prays daily and who has given her life to Christ.

For my daughter, that moment was as priceless as the day I prayed for my sister's healing. Teach your children to pray.

Now, there are times when God answers prayers but not always in the way we would expect. Still, God will give us wisdom about how to handle that. My friend Darlene taught her son to pray for people when he was a little boy, just as I taught my daughter. He would go to bed at night and call the people by name. Many, facing significant health challenges, would be encouraged by his prayers. When they met him, they thanked him. And this encouraged him to pray even more. We pray for things, and we hope what we pray for comes to fruition.

As you read this, I encourage you to pray and see the salvation of the Lord. What is the most powerful

prayer you ever prayed? Describe the results. Describe a prayer you prayed when you did not get the answer you prayed for?

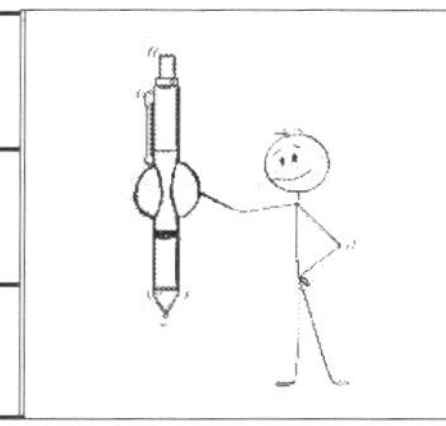

CHAPTER 6

HOPED FOR

Hebrews 11:1 says "faith is the substance of things *hoped for.*" I will talk about faith in the next chapter. But now, I want to focus on hope. I always saw the two connected. I even wondered how anyone could have hope but no faith. Is that even possible? Then, I realized people with hope and no faith must find themselves in a lonely place.

I have shared my experiences in the previous chapters where I prayed, and I hoped that the answers would come. I was looking for *the evidence* of my hope. According to Wikipedia,

hope is defined as *an optimistic attitude of mind that is based on an expectation of positive outcomes related to events and circumstances in one's life or the world at large.* Note: the operative words here are 'positive outcomes' and 'optimistic attitudes.' (https://en.m.wikepedia.org/wiki/Hope)

I have never gone into a prayer situation where I did not expect a positive outcome. Even when my parents were sick and in hospice, I remained hopeful hoping they would live. After all, I had hoped Dede would live, and she did. I hoped Lowesie would get healed, and he did. I hoped Isaiah would walk, and he did. Surely, hoping my dad and mom would be healed and live wasn't an unrealistic expectation. So, I hoped and hoped and hoped as I prayed and prayed and prayed. But this time, what I hoped for, I didn't get. I didn't experience the evidence. For a moment in time, I felt hopeless. Not seeing the evidence made me question my hope and, ultimately, my faith. I felt lost and thought: *How do I get my hope back? Where did it go?*

1 Thessalonians 1:3 reminds us that we have to *have a patience of hope in Jesus.*

Yeah, I sure needed that patience because I do become impatient when I want something and expect it.

What always amazed me was watching a child with great hope for something they desire. They jump around excited to the point that you can't contain them. Have you ever observed a kid waiting to open presents? How they rip open the box, having paper flying everywhere, as soon as they get the chance. But when they get the box opened and inside is something they didn't want, notice the face. The burst bubble of expectation is shown all over them. Kids don't have filters. If they genuinely don't like something, they keep it moving. And some will even say they didn't get what they wanted.

However, when that box contains what they really hoped for, they often are so excited that they can't contain themselves. Some scream. Some shout. Some dance. Some say, "Thank you!" But most, if not all, take their expected gift and run to a place where they can enjoy it. Well, that is how we are with God. Or maybe I should say that is how *I was* and, in some instances, still am.

The higher the expectation of my hope, the more profound my disappointment when I don't get what I hoped for. I have a hard time pretending that I am happy. Even when I knew God didn't allow me to experience the evidence of that hope for a reason, I still struggled to find contentment. I have had to learn to keep my hope even when I don't see the evidence.

†

Now, when I have hoped for something, and it comes, like a kid I get all giddy inside. I can't wait to tell someone how blessed I was to get exactly what I hoped for. And it's moments like these that fuel my continuous hope experiences. Seeing the evidence of my hope has increased my faith walk and my faith experience.

As I further ponder the true meaning and example of hope in my life, I reflect on three succinct experiences, which by no means represent detailed hope illustrations in my life.

The first occurred in January 1987. My oldest daughter was just one month shy of her first birthday. My husband and I lived in a little town named Menands, NY. Across from our apartment were former NBA Player Kenny Natt and his wife, Jolene. Jolene was a nurse and worked overnight. She was pregnant and had previously miscarried and was having a hard time. Our husbands, who played in the Continental Basketball Association (CBA), were out of town on a road trip. Jolene came home one morning and was very upset as she was spotting. We talked, and I could see her worry in her eyes and as a mother of what she so desperately wanted, I could feel her pain. But all I could do was cry with her. There was a dumpster outside and she kept an eye on my Michie while I took out our garbage. As I walked to the dumpster, tears began to fall even harder from my eyes and I cried out to God. I said, "Lord, please make sure everything is alright with my friend. All she wants is to have her baby. Please, Lord, if I never have another child, give her this child." My plea was so strong that my throat ached as I talked. I didn't want her to know what I had prayed, so I got myself together before returning to the house. I hoped and prayed and prayed and hoped that God would perform a miracle. And

God did more than that. Jolene held on to her miracle baby; she was born in July of that year. Also, my second child was born ten months later. Both are beautiful women in their thirties today, and Jolene and Kenny now have two daughters. They all are substance and evidence of what we all hoped for.

I further pondered on hope. Fast forward to 2018. My oldest daughter Michelle was an accomplished woman at this point in her life. She was one of the youngest Principals in the NYC School District. I watched her heart broken on a couple of occasions and as a mom, my heart broke for her. But I couldn't protect her from it as much as I wanted to. So, I did what I knew to do. I hoped and then prayed that God would bless her with a good husband who would love her from her soul. One night, I stood outside in front of my house after walking my dog. I looked to the heavens and began sharing my hope and prayer to God for my daughter. I felt this warmth come over me. The response was, "He's right under her nose." I said nothing to her; I just continued to pray. Little did I know she had rekindled a relationship with a young man she had dated four years prior. This time, he fell in love with her soul and by 2019, they were married. As of the writing of this book, they have two children and are an example of the substance of my hope turned to prayer. I learned to hope and pray for my children. This feeling burns inside me as I always hope for what's best for them. As God did with Jolene and Kenny, he also did this time. Not only did that hope and prayer come true for Michelle and my son-in-love Dakarai, it also came true for my daughter Shireyll as she married her soulmate, Steve, three years later. As of this book's writing, they will soon be parents.

Hope endured even further in 2020. My husband and I longed to be grandparents. Our Godson (who became our son) gave us a granddaughter Amaya in 2014. She's #1. However, we continued to hope for more.

What we didn't know was in September 2019, our daughter Michelle experienced a miscarriage. She and her husband didn't tell anyone. On Christmas Day 2019, they surprised our family with an announcement that they would become parents in June. The excitement of what we had hoped for overwhelmed me with tears. It was finally going to happen. Then, my daughter told me they had waited a while to mention this to us because she had already had a miscarriage, and they wanted to get beyond the risk. I, unfortunately, began to perseverate over what Michelle said about miscarriage. I worried about her every move. My hope began to shake. One night in January 2020, while I was in the same place where I had hoped and prayed for my daughter to find a good husband, I found myself hoping for a healthy grandbaby. I had a similar cry out with Jolene and Kenny but not those exact words. I began trying to visualize holding my new grandchild. I didn't know if it would be a boy or a girl. I looked to the heavens and asked God to take the worry away. I hoped for a safe delivery and no miscarriage. Then I heard a voice say, "GiGi (my name given to me by AMAYA) stop worrying; you will see me soon." I felt the same warmth I felt previously. I was familiar with it. Worry left and hope and anticipation took the lead. Two months later, our country and world experienced a pandemic CORONAVIRUS 19.

People were dying by the thousands. My daughter was pregnant and my hope persevered through fear. On June 18, 2020, the substance of my hope appeared as a beautiful baby boy named Dakotah. My heart exploded. Yes, KotiBear, your words came true. You will see me soon. My life has never been the same. And just like God did when I prayed for Jolene and Kenny's lil girl, God did it again. In October 2021, my son Jamayal and his wife Joi added Jade to our family as they made Amaya a big sister. Three days later, Dakotah became a big brother when Hartley was born. Hope endured. Hope continues to take hold, as Lanie is due to enter as the fourth grandchild born during the pandemic.

As you read my hope journey, I am sure the substance of what you hoped for is flooding your thoughts, and you may remember feeling disappointed at not having received all you hoped. That is the nature of hope. We may or may not get what we hope for, but can we still love God; can we still put our hope in Him? I hoped and prayed my parents would live, they didn't, but I won't stop hoping and praying. Don't ever give up hope. It fuels and drives our faith. My prayer for you today is that your hope will endure and that, ultimately, your faith will increase. And if God does with this hope and prayer as he has done with the others, you will receive an overflow of blessings and results. Hope my substance.

What does hope mean to you? What are you hoping for today?

CHAPTER 7

FAITH IS

Hebrews 11:1 says that faith is the substance of things hoped for and the evidence of things not seen, and **Hebrews 11:2** says for by it the Elders received a good report.

James 2:20 asks the question is faith without works dead.... And in **James 26**, the answer comes back that it is dead, without works.

So, what is faith with works?

Deductive reasoning would lead us to think, it is *alive* or *living*. Faith comes with some type of action. It is not a standalone word.

People will ask, "Do you have faith?"

"Where is your faith?"

They'll say, "Faith don't fail me now. Oh, ye of little faith." Faith is an often-used word in the life of a believer.

Examine how you have used this word. Have you used it in conjunction with outcomes or a precipitant to expectations? Do you use it connected to hope? How is faith connected in your life?

I learned about faith at a very young age. It came right along with hope and prayer for me. I didn't realize that my experience surrounding my sister had anything to do with my faith. I also did not realize that the outcome of my prayer strengthened my faith. But it did.

Read the second chapter in the book of James. This chapter discusses faith and the working of faith. How does one profess faith and see people poor and hungry and do nothing? How does the working of that faith produce fruit or evidence thereof? What does the assertion 'Faith without works is dead' mean to you?

____

____

____

____

____

____

____

†

My experiences over the years have caused my faith to increase. Watching God do His handiwork in my life and the lives of those I know is amazing. But my faith has also increased by immersing myself in the Word of God, listening to preaching, and teaching. My husband says (and he heard it from another gentleman) that if you're the smartest person in the room, get into a new room.

The Word in **Romans 10:17** tells us, "Faith cometh by hearing and hearing by the Word of God."

How can they hear except there be a preacher, and how can one preach lest he be sent?" So, if you want your faith to increase, hear what the Spirit is saying to the church. *We* are the church. I can honestly say, had I not had enough Word in me, I don't think I could have made it through my storms and tests.

I am somewhat fascinated by people who don't believe in God. There are some that I know, and I have asked, "Why don't you believe?"

They say things like, "If there is a God, why would He do *this or that*?"

I've said, "Do you ask man why he does *this or that*?"

Many things people complain about were not done by God but by man. God allowed Adam and Eve to eat the fruit by giving them the ability to make choices and have free will. Similarly, He has also done that with us today. The consequences we face result from our actions. God permits us to act outside of His will. But when we align our will with God's will, the blessing is amazing. I have seen many marriages fail and struggle because people choose their will versus God's. But that's a whole other book. I can tell you some stories.

Another reason people don't believe in God

(and that is not about God either) is about the representatives of God. Some people only see the God in us. So, if we say we have God in us and are mean-spirited, gossipers, backbiters, whoremongers, thieves, and liars, why would people even believe God exists?

My faith in Jesus Christ came along with my realization that He was there with me all the time. When I look thoroughly over my life, I can reflect on instances when He was there. His presence hovered over me when I was right and even when I was wrong. Today, I thank Him for blessing me, and I thank Him for not punishing me when I was wrong. But my faith, *my* faith, my *faith* reminds me that my Intercessor stands in the visual path of God who no longer sees me but sees my sin cleansed life on His righteous Son.

Faith moved mountains out of my way. Faith allowed me to walk in the midst of chaos and focus on Jesus so I could rise above the fray. Faith allowed me to see beyond the *now* to my *next.* Faith taught me to love through my hate when people treated me badly. Faith made me learn to believe the outcome before it happened. Faith made me experience and expect the supernatural . . . faith.

I believe and expect to get even better in my faith walk. One of my favorite biblical expressions of faith is when the three Hebrew boys were about to be tossed into the fiery furnace, and they responded that they believed God was able to deliver them, but if He didn't, they still would not bow down to any golden image. That's faith!

The Bible tells us we should not waver in our faith. I have to be honest. When my mom died, my faith wavered. I didn't really realize how weak I was. My knees shook, and my heart stopped beating for a moment. I didn't even realize that prior to her death but my faith was more in her than in God.

†

Let Me Explain.

I was definitely *not* a mama's girl. I was a *daddy's girl.* My dad was the absolute man of my life; the first man I ever loved. My mom took a definite back seat to him. What I realize today and loved most about her was she didn't even mind. She knew how I felt because she was a daddy's girl, too. I had it so bad that after my dad, *my hero*, died, every time I looked in the mirror, I saw him in my face.

Now, most people said when I was growing up (and even now) that I looked like my mom, but all I ever saw in my face after my dad died was him. One day, I told my mom a story about how much I looked like my dad. She had a way of chuckling, which made the hearer know she thought the statement was cute but not true. It took three years after my dad died for me to realize I actually did look like my mom. Prior to my dad dying, I called him on the phone just about every day on my way to work. He would always say two things in his very deep voice, "Patrice, this is your Father" (like I did not know that) and "God Loves You, and So Do I." How I miss that!

In 2013, I decided that on my 50th Birthday, I would cut my hair, so I could take a picture with my mom to see how much we looked alike. By then, I was skinny like her, and my features began to resemble her even more. But I didn't cut my hair all the way short like hers. I cut mine shoulder-length. My *new* hero and I had talked almost every morning following my dad's transition. My mom, who had been critical at times when I was young, had become one of my biggest supporters. When I would preach, she would leave her church and come to hear me. She would tell me she was proud of me.

I began to seek her advice as often as I could. My mom was a social worker. I never wanted to be a social worker. My baby sister became a social worker before I did, and eventually, I succumbed to the social work bug. That made my connection to my mom even greater. Hers was a soft voice that garnered much power in the field of social work. She was instrumental in New York State getting licensure. Because she took my sister and me to an event to get the state legislators to vote on the licensure law, we were all honored. Yep, my mom was pretty awesome, and she was beautiful on the inside and out. Every time I was hit with a work challenge, I would call my mom first. I didn't go to God and seek His guidance or His will for my life. If God wanted to speak to me about my job, He had to speak with my mother first. *What? Ask God? Pray? Who me?* Nah, I just asked my mom.

And thus, my faith took a big blow to its foundational core on October 15th, 2013. My mom lasted only six weeks after her cancer diagnosis. She didn't fight, or at least that is what I thought. I prayed from the day I heard the diagnosis. I believed God would heal her or at least give us more time. *Who would I talk to? Who was going to answer my questions? Who, God? Who?* And that is why my faith was shaken. I am not saying we shouldn't ask our parents things. But to put it in perspective, we should ask God first, then our parents. We need to lay a foundation and create a habit of speaking with God.

One day, not long after my mom died, I was having an angry moment with God. I was in the shower, and I was really struggling. Tears were flowing, and I felt the need to question God. *Who did I really think I was?* As the water hit my face, tears flowed along with the water into my mouth when I asked God, "Why did You let my mom die? I was obedient to Your call. I attended prayer. I attended Bible Class. I worshiped You and praised You. Lord, why didn't You hear me?"

Finally, I screamed, "Why didn't YOU answer my prayers?!!!"

As clear as my yell, I heard God say, "Because I answered hers."

It was at that very moment I realized and accepted that my mom was ready. And as much as I was praying for her to stay, she was praying to be released into our Savior's arms. I washed my face and stopped crying. I realized that it wasn't about me or my will. I had to grow up. I was 50 years old, and it was time for me to 'grow up.' I had no parents left. I had no one I could call on like my mom.

Thanks be to God for the other mothers in my life—Mother Dixon, my godmother Betty, and my godmother Evelyn! But it was my awesome mother-in-love, Jeannette McNair, who told me she would be my mom now. She has been that ever since. I sure do love that woman! And I now talk to my sister daily, and we often laugh about things my mom did that we could write stories about.

I loved my mom, but I know my kids love me the same way. They call me just like I called my mom. But I want them to seek God, too. As a matter of fact, seek God first and seek Him more. When they come *to me*, I also go to God for their answers. One day, as I was looking through my mom's papers, I found prayers she wrote to God for us. All this time, I was going to her, and all this time, she was going to God.

CHAPTER 8

GOOD NEWS

In biblical Greek, the word **oida**, means "to have knowledge of." In the study of *Kingdom Agenda*, Dr. Tony Evans describes oida, as knowing something even when you don't really know. Evans further references **Romans 8:28**, which is to *know* that "all things work together for good to them who love God to those who are the called according to his purpose." To *know* when you really don't know, but you just feel it; if you have that level of faith, you will *know* that it will be *good*. It is also described in an article by Darby the describes the difference between two types of knowledge, ginosko and oida. Oida is objective knowledge and ginosko is relational knowledge based on experience. I have both oida and ginosko knowledge of God. I know what I know, and I know who I know.

I remember early in ministry, I preached a message that said, "It's All Good." I used Joseph and his experience where he was thrown in the pit by his brothers because they were jealous of his relationship with his father, Jacob. They meant evil upon him, but Joseph, the dreamer, became all that he dreamed. He became the number two man to Pharaoh and was positioned to save his family later in life. The major scripture in this passage says, **Genesis 50:20** "As for you, you meant evil against me, but God meant *good* in order to bring about this present result, to preserve many people alive." There are some experiences we endure that make us feel like we are under the attack of the enemy and are losing. But I have had enough experiences and the relationship with God to have oida, knowing that if I just hold on, *good* will come of it.

I wanted this book to not just be a testimony where tears might be shed, but also a flight into understanding the need to persevere and to know that good *will* prevail over evil.

I love studying Tony Evans's *Kingdom Agenda.* He reminds us that people are intrigued by the battle of good versus evil. Many television shows and movies have us captivated by the good versus evil mentality. They will have ugly villains and beautiful heroes. There are princes, princesses, kings, and queens who prevail. These things flood our minds with hope and give us a sense that (1) the enemy will keep coming after us, but (2) good *will* win. I will win, devil you will lose. I will make it.

Jesus reminded the people that He came to preach *The Good News*. And that is what we are to do today. We must preach *The Good News*. It doesn't mean we ignore the bad news, but somehow, we have to see the glass half full. I always say I am going to see the glass full and overflowing. Because once you give me a glass half full, I am going to fill it up even more.

Good news makes you want to smile, laugh, dance, sing, praise, and shout. It makes you feel good inside. It makes hormones release endorphins into your bloodstream. We have to reach a place where if and when someone tries to flood us with bad news, we can respond by flooding them with good news. Now, I am still practicing that. We must practice good, because it is our nature to fall in to negativity.

I was sharing with my Bible class that as I was paying attention to what the Lord over my life was saying to me, I heard something that shifted my thinking. Now, all of you biblical scholars may take umbrage with what I am saying; just remember this was my conversation with God. God gave me divine assignments to counsel some people. My profession is social work, and I have been an executive in a substance use disorder treatment program for 19 years (when I initially wrote this and now, for over 22 years). I have a master's degree, and for the most part, I think I am relatively smart. So, when these assignments came my way, I figured my smarts could handle them. Of course, I have studied, I have experience, and I can handle this. *Right?* Nope.

At some point, I said, "God why are you sending me these issues, and you know I am going to fail?" God laughed at my complaint. Then He took me to a very familiar story in the bible. I will share it here, like He gave it to me.

God: Patrice.... Do you remember the story in the bible about Adam and Eve?

Me: Yes, God. I do.

God: Do you remember how I put this beautiful garden together, created the animals, and created Adam? I even gave Adam a woman that I made from his rib? You remember that story right Patrice?

Me: Yes, God. (I wanted God to hurry along, but He took His time.)

God: Well, I put two trees in the garden, and I told Adam he could eat from one but not the other. The one he could eat from was the *Tree of Life*, and the one he couldn't eat from was the *Tree of Knowledge of Good and Evil.* You remember that, right?

Me: Yes, God (sounding exasperated).

God: Well, the woman I made for Adam ended up in a conversation with a serpent who was Satan in disguise, and he convinced her through trickery to eat from the wrong tree. She made a choice.... And then she (not the serpent) gave the fruit to Adam. Do you remember?

Me: Yes, God, what is your point?

God: Be patient, my dear, because you know that is your weakness. I want you to get this point and get it clearly. I had to remove the *Tree of Life* from them because now, they would think they were smarter than I was. They would try to get ideas like Lucifer did in Isaiah 14 when he thought he would ascend high above the clouds and mountains. They would think their knowledge was greater than my gift.

Me: (Nodding and beginning to tear up)

God: You see, you have this knowledge that you received from school. You are smart, indeed. But these problems I gave you *cannot* be solved . . . with just your knowledge.

Your social work practices cannot solve these issues. These issues are bigger than that. These problems will be solved by eating from the *Tree of Life*.

God: In other words, you need to seek Jesus Christ for your answers. You need to fast and pray for these issues. They are deeply rooted and not easily shaken. Eat from the right *Tree.*

Don't you know that the *Tree of Life* already possesses all the knowledge you will ever need? Listen, Patrice, when people get a diagnosis from a doctor, one of the first things they do is try to go to man's knowledge. They go on the internet and pull up signs and symptoms of the diagnosis and the potential prognosis. Many have themselves in the casket before they even come to me. Patrice, teach them to seek me first. Patrice, let them know to come to the *Tree of Life*.

Me: (Now, I was totally crying because this was so me). Yes, Lord! I will. I will. I will.

God: Good, daughter. One last thing. In my Word, it is written that *faith* without works is dead. So then, what is faith with works?

Me: Life?

God: It is the *Tree of Life*, and that *Tree* now is Jesus. Now, go tell them *The Good News*. The *Tree* still brings forth life.

Me: Yes, God! Yes!

†

So, I come to share good news with you. No matter what you are going through…no matter what you are experiencing…focus on the good. Jesus said in Luke that He was bringing *The Good News* to the poor. *Good News* to the poor means provision. The funny thing is, while I am yet typing this, I am physically feeling sick. My head aches, I am nauseous, dizzy, and I think I have a fever. But God!

I am on a mission. Have you ever been in the midst of your *go through* and right there, right in the middle you begin to think of how good God is? I mean, on the inside, you feel His presence, and *you know* that no matter how crazy things get, God is still *good*, and He is still *able*. Just think how it must have been for Shadrach, Meshach, and Abednego **(Daniel 3)** when they were getting ready to be tossed into the fiery furnace. Anyone else would be trying to escape. At least, I would be, because I hate fire. They probably would have had to kill me before tossing me in…. But they just insisted that they would not bow to Nebuchadnezzar's commands and that God was *able* to deliver them. See, we have to get like that! We have to believe God is *able* no matter what fire we are about to enter. Attitude has so much to do with it...*Sow What.*

†

My coworker and friend Joanne was diagnosed with stage 4 colon cancer in 2005. From day, one her attitude was I am not dying until I am ready. Not long after her diagnosis, she came to my church... a little Catholic white lady walked into a Black Pentecostal church and came to the front of the church during prayer time. Our Co-Pastor, Elder Mother Dorothy Dixon, asked Joanne if it was ok to put oil on her head. Joanne said, "You could put Crisco or STP on me if it is going to work." Joanne raised her hands, and Mother prayed the prayer of faith.

The two must have been on the same page with God because Joanne walked out of there on cloud nine with her chin in the air and her arms swinging side to side behind her like George Jefferson. "I got prayed for," she exclaimed. Later that month, she declared she would paint one toenail for each year she lived beyond cancer. Her stage four cancer required removing her colon and part of her liver. She later had additional surgeries. But her attitude never wavered. As of the final writing of this book, Joanne is eighteen years past that initial experience and still has that same fight and swagger. Oh, and all of her toes are red. She never forgot *The Good News* that was prayed in her ears. Today, she tells everyone of her good news.

How about you? Do you have good news to share? Encourage someone today with some *Good News*.... It will make you feel much better than sharing bad news.

CHAPTER 9

VICTORY IS MINE

Now, if you have been to church before, an upbeat hymn may immediately come to mind. Victory, however, should not be an afterthought but a forethought. In other words, if we woke up each day proclaiming victory over our lives, how we would approach the day would change. Understanding that every day the enemy seeks to make sure we are losers and not winners, we should wake up with a victorious attitude.

My sister tells me all the time that I am *very* competitive. Truth be told, I am. But as much as I compete against others, I compete with myself. I am always trying to do better the next time and get to the next level. You have my attention if you give me anything with numbers or letters to try to figure out. I believe in being victorious.

As a young girl, I was an athlete. I played any sport I could. My dad was an assistant principal at Hawthorne Middle School in Yonkers when I was first introduced to sports. I would go and watch Charlie Criss and Bernard Toone play basketball. I would sit with the cheerleaders and cheer. Somehow, I switched my desires from *cheering for people* to *wanting to feel* what it was like to have people to cheer for me. So, I took to sports. I started running track at the Police Athletic League (PAL) in Yonkers, NY. I loved it and had so many trophies my parents had to put a bookshelf in my room to hold them. I polished them often. Next, was football but that was on the block—Seneca Avenue. I was like the little girl from *Remember the Titans* who loved football. I knew and still know, the penalties, the plays—everything. I even taught the little boys on the block how to play. When they became men, they loved telling people *a girl* taught them how to play. Next, I found softball. I played in 8th grade with my cousin on a women's team. That was fun, but I never picked it up again after that summer. That is because my next sport became my absolute favorite, basketball.

I started watching basketball with my dad when I was young. My favorite player was Walt "Clyde" Frazier. By the time I got to high school, I had already been a pretty good player. I joined a team of girls from Mount Vernon after spending K-8 grades in Yonkers. And if I wasn't already competitive enough, my Mount Vernon team won every game in ninth grade, and I remember one game when the opponent's team only scored two points. My new teammates became my lifelong friends and fueled my competitive desires even more. We lost very few games over the next two years, but once we became seniors, we never lost again. We won the first New York State Public High School Girls Championship 26-0. A feat that, as of the writing of this book, has not been repeated by any Girls Basketball team at our High School. Being part of a successful team taught me so many things. When I became an adult, I returned to my high school and became a coach. By then, my competitive nature was even worse.

The problem with my competitive nature is that I always have been so driven that I had to learn how to lose *and not* crumble. I wanted to be victorious all the time. So, learning how to regroup after losing was not easy. I learned this more as a coach than I ever did as a player. Even when I ran track in high school during my first two years, my 1-mile relay team was victorious. And we set a record that lasted 25 years! Once I began working in my regular job, I kept my competitive spirit. I often tell people if you want to be a winner, hang on because I don't lose often. But I owe all this to God's anointed favor over my life. The many successes I've experienced fuel my persistence and perseverance. Now, I hate losing so much that if I know I am going to lose, I will give in or concede. Notice I said *give in* and not *give up*. Be assured if I get the opportunity to regroup, I will.

My need to win was evident in elementary school, middle school, high school, college; it is still in me today. So, when the enemy comes for me, I see it as a competitive challenge. But I had to learn not to try to fight the enemy alone. I had to learn that *to win* I had to enlist my power source. **Philippians 4:13** says, "I can do all things through Christ who strengthens me." See, that is when my powers became unleashed. **Luke 10:19** says, "Behold I have given you power to tread over serpents and scorpions and over all the power of the enemy: and nothing shall by any means hurt you." The more I realized that Christ has provided me with a power transfer, the more I realized that no matter the challenge, I would be victorious.

When I was a little girl at the Church of Our Savior in Yonkers, we sang the hymn, "We Are Climbing Jacob's Ladder." I'd later realize that, like in the hymn, the stronger I became in my Christian walk, the harder the enemy's devices came at me. Every round became more intense. The enemy came harder, but my Superpower, Jesus Christ, in the form of the Holy Spirit, came harder and stronger. I say all this to encourage you.

I invite you to listen to the song by Meaghan Williams, "I Made It," which says it all. No weapon formed against me shall prosper! I will win. He will lose. Stay strong, and stay in the fight. And remember what God told Jehoshaphat when the children of Judah went to battle against multiple armies. This battle is *not* yours. It's the Lord's!

Finally, I want to share this one story about a victory that shares my absolute philosophy of life. In 1992, Derek Redmond, a British Olympian sprinter, was running the 400 meters. With less than 200 meters away, he pulled his hamstring and fell to the ground. His father saw his son in distress, came down from the bleachers, and jumped on the track. He ran to his son's aid. Instead of staying on the ground, the son asked his father to bring him to the finish line. His father put his arm around his son, and together they made it across the line. Now, Derek finished last, but he finished, and he didn't finish alone! His father came to his rescue, and our Father will come to our rescue when the enemy tries to prevent us from winning our race. Derek was victorious, and we will be too!

That is exactly how I felt when my son was coming through his illness and ran track for the first time after one year of torture and treatments. When he came in last, I was at the finish line, filled with tears. It wasn't about winning anymore. It was about finishing. I learned that finishing was winning. I pray this story encourages you to stay in the fight. Finish. Win. But don't give up. At least not to your enemy. Give it all to your Superpower. That is *how* I win every day!

What was your most memorable victory and what did it you have to endure to get it? Did you ever lose to win?

CHAPTER 10

THE POWER OF YOUR TESTIMONY

Revelation 21:11

[11]*They triumphed over him by the blood of the Lamb and by the word of their testimony; they did not love their lives so much as to shrink from death.*

Psalms 119:46

[46]*I will speak of thy testimonies also before kings, and will not be ashamed.*

I have often wondered: why me? *Why me, Lord?* Have you ever felt that way before? Have you ever asked God what did you ever do to deserve an experience? Well, I realized that God allowed me to experience my *go through,* so I could go through, so I could tell you. I know that seems confusing, but one of my favorite scriptures is one that I heard for the first time from Pastor John Massey in Troy, NY. **1 Corinthians 10:13** says,

> [13] *There hath no temptation taken you but such as is common to man: but God is faithful, who will not suffer you to be tempted above that ye are able; but will with the temptation also make a way to escape, that ye may be able to bear it.*

I often keep that scripture in mind when I am fighting through tough situations. *He will make a way of escape.* I am also encouraged by the last part of **Luke 10:19**, which states, *"and nothing shall by any means hurt you."* These scriptures fuel my testimony. God *is* faithful, He *will* make a way of escape, and nothing shall hurt me. Well, now that last part requires clarification.

I have been hurt. But the hurt referenced in this scripture was more than just my hurt feelings. This hurt meant nothing could hurt my soul. Just like in the book of **Job**, when Satan approached God's throne (**Job 1:6** and **Job 2:1**), and God introduced Job into the conversation: *Have you considered my servant Job* (**Job 1:8** and **Job 2:3**)? God told Satan he could go after Job, but he couldn't touch his life. When it was all said and done, God gave Job a testimony.

†

A **testimony** by definition, is a public recounting of a religious conversion or experience. The testimony I am referring to is mostly experienced. This book is a culmination of my testimonial experiences. I wrote them to encourage others and remind myself of how good my God is. I want to encourage you, as well. *Write it down and make it plain.* As I said in the beginning, I first started writing this book in 2008. The funny thing about that is I also started writing a book about my son Isaiah then, too. It was called *The Perfect Butterfly*. I completed that in 2014, and it is an awesome testimonial, depicted in an illustrative poem.

In 2000, the kids in the neighborhood were outside playing. They were running around my front yard. Isaiah came to me and asked if he could go outside and play with the kids. Fearing he would get hurt, I said no. With a sad face he looked at me with tears and said, “Well, can I sit in the window and look at them?”

That hit me right in my gut. All special needs children were assigned social workers from the county. Later that week, when his social worker came to see him, I told her the story. Betty, his social worker, told me about a basketball team at Westchester United Cerebral Palsy called the Barrier Breakers. My husband and I, being former basketball players, were so excited. We took Isaiah to play. He could play and no longer had to remain inside. He became an awesome basketball player and won MVP in several tournaments.

In 2008, my cousin Judy took Isaiah to all of his wheelchair basketball games. He was playing for the *Long Island Lightning* team, and they were very good. Their team traveled to many places to play, including Maryland, Philadelphia, New Jersey, Kentucky, etc. Judy was a Godsend for my husband and me. Many people didn't even know I was his mother. They thought Judy was his mother because she went with him everywhere. I was working two jobs then, trying to keep money coming in and food on the table. My husband was also working and had been taking our kids to events.

Mother's Day was approaching, and I asked Judy what she liked. She said butterflies. (Ironically, my mom used to call me 'Butterfly.') Nevertheless, Robin Kett, a lady at my job, took pictures. I asked her if she had any photos of butterflies, and she told me she didn't. A week or so later, she came into my office excited, carrying a lot of pictures in her hand. She spread them on the table, and there were butterflies everywhere. I was so excited! And then I noticed she kept moving one of the pictures away and apologizing. So, I said, "What's wrong?"

She said, "Well, I didn't realize this until later, but one of the butterflies had a hole in its wing. It is messing up the pictures."

I saw she had several photographs with that butterfly alone. I started to cry and grabbed the butterfly picture with the hole in the wing. I said, "That is the picture I want!"

She looked baffled. She asked, "Why?"

I explained that my son was born with spina bifida, which means he was born with a hole in his spine. I also shared that many people would see him as imperfect, but he was the most perfect gift for me. And this butterfly is the most perfect gift for my cousin Judy. I asked if I could hang onto the pictures. She agreed. I put the pictures in a particular order and wrote this poem.

The Perfect Butterfly

One day, as I was driving along,
I happened on a barn.
I said to myself, "What a picture!"

From the purple flowers I saw afar.

As I drew closer to the colorful sea,
Holding my camera tight,
A butterfly floated from its rest,
And something engulfed my sight.

Not one, two, three, or four . . .
But five butterflies in one space!
I gasped for air, as I clicked and clicked
To capture God's purple place,

And when I got home to view the scene,
One picture at a time,
I noticed something I did not see
With my naked eye.

One butterfly had a broken wing.
Look there's the hole!
I'll show the picture anyway, but
I'm sure it won't be sold.

Picture after picture, the hole
It filled the lot.
How can I sell any of them
With that one dark spot?

But, to a mom I showed the pictures,
And with tears she stared and stared.
She said, "That is the one that I want!
It shows God really cares."

I asked, "Can you tell me please what you see?
Cause I just see this hole!"
She said, "But then, God placed him on this

bush.
And the purple made him whole."

It's all in how you look at things, and
When God is in your life,
He'll make imperfection perfect. He can
Make what's wrong turn right.

See my son has a hole in his back, and
As imperfect as he may seem,
God filled him with His agape love.
So that he, too, may dream!

So, when I saw this butterfly,
I did not see his hole.
I saw God's purple presence
Capturing my soul!!!!

This poem, accompanied by her pictures, catalyzed my first book. Because this book is in black and white, the printing cannot capture its beauty. However, what came next was even more evidence of *why*.

Why did you allow me to go through this stuff, God? What do you want me to do?

He answered, "Tell them. Tell them of your journey. Someone may be encouraged to stay in the fight. Someone may be encouraged to tell their story, too. There can never be enough stories."

So, I began to tell my story every chance I got. Whenever I heard of a mother who birthed a child with special needs or was raising one with special needs, I became inspired. Little did I know how much it would impact my own church? We are a small church with many children born with health issues or who later experience health issues. After Isaiah was born and I experienced what I did with Lowesie, I learned that my godson Travis was on the Autism spectrum. Then, another boy from my church, who has playfully called me "Mommy" since he was little, was diagnosed with Childhood Diabetes. A third child was diagnosed with Childhood Diabetes, and my youngest godson is also on the Autism Spectrum. Still, another was diagnosed with narcolepsy, and another with childhood cancer. Lastly, my nephew is my godson, and he has a baby girl; she was born with cysts on her brain, is visually impaired, and is developmentally delayed.

I would have missed much of this testimony if I had written this book sooner. I have been able to be there and available for almost every one of these mothers because I have already seen, felt, and experienced their fears, devastation, and despair.

†

Travis and Mikey

I remember sharing with Travis's mom, Marion, how it felt watching other kids born around the same time as Isaiah experience their developmental milestones while Isaiah's development was lagging.

She then said to me, "Well, at least your son can spontaneously say, 'I love you.'"

"Wow," I thought to myself. Sometimes you think you got problems and someone else is going through, too. So, I proceeded to tell my godson every time I saw him, "Aunt Trice loves you!"

He used to say back, "Aunt Trice loves you!"

Then, I changed it to "Aunt Trice loves me!"

He would then say, "Aunt Trice loves me!"

One day, he said, "Travis loves you!" And even later, he said, "I love you, Aunt Trice." And I got the biggest hug and kiss spontaneously.

Needless to say, this guy has my heart. What a testimony of great faith and perseverance! Oh, and he said to his mom, "Aunt Trice wrote a book for Isaiah. Is she going to write a book about me?" (Of course, you know I did.) It has been completed, and his poem is called, "Finding My Roar." It is about a Lion who had to find his voice, much like Travis and Mikey (my other godson on the spectrum). In 2023, Mikey read this poem to his teacher for an assignment, and all I could do was cry. In the same month, Travis was the keynote speaker for Autism Awareness Month at a special event. These boys just melt my heart.

I forgot to mention two very critical components about both Travis and Mikey. Travis's mom, Marion, is Isaiah's godmother. She is the one who prayed me through when Isaiah had his second surgery and when doctors gave Lowesie that diagnosis that devastated me. Now, it was my turn to encourage her. Lena is Mikey's mom. When Isaiah was born with all of his challenges, Lena told me right when I brought him home that he would be the ring bearer in her wedding. We had a lot of boys born that year. I couldn't imagine her letting a paralyzed boy be her ringbearer. She had really just started dating the guy she was with. Three years later, my son had just started walking, and he *was* the *RINGBEARER* for Lena and Mike's wedding. We became Mikey's godparents, and as Lena and Mike experience their challenges as parents, they have our attention, love, and support. Today, Travis is a college graduate, and Mikey is in junior high school. I am so proud of both of them, but they have an even greater story to tell.

My godson, Mychal, was born six weeks before Isaiah. He was this handsome baby, the young boy who played every sport, and an intelligent kid. He met his developmental milestones early, and it was hard watching that, knowing my son was not thriving the same way. But I had to learn to appreciate the successes when they came. Isaiah didn't begin walking until age three after doctors told us he would *never* walk. He struggled in school and had to fight to go from the 'D' honor roll to the 'B' honor roll. I say the "D" honor roll with all sincerity. My son would work so hard to pass his tests and could not retain information. So, we had to learn to reward his progress incrementally. By the time he was in 8th grade with my father (the educator) tutoring him, he had made the 'B' honor roll. He stayed there through high school. Mychal had his share of challenges through high school, but to me, he was and still is my handsome nephew/godson, whom I love dearly. By the time he was 19, he was the father of the cutest little girl, Maleah. His little girl's birth and health challenges usurped all of his developmental milestones. She had several surgeries on her brain to insert and repair a shunt. She had a hard time keeping food down and stabilizing her sodium. She was unable to see except for bright colors. But this beautiful baby was and still is amazing.

†

Maleah's Story

In April 2017, after returning from Charlotte, NC, my 98-year-old aunt had just had her hip replaced following a fall. That was a miracle in and of itself. I watched my aunt learn how to walk again with a walker, and when that happened, I cried. The doctors thought she would not make it through the surgery, but she had God on her side.

The day I returned home, it was a Sunday, and I walked into the Boys and Girls Club of Mount Vernon, where my family was in the gym. I saw Maleah with a toy that looked like a walker. She was holding on to it and walking. Then, she let it go and started to walk. I had never seen her do that before, so I was a basket of tears. Because she did not have good vision, it was hard to keep her balance, and she would rock back and forth. And then, she would fall. But she would crawl to the vicinity of the bright-colored toy, pull herself up laughing, and try it again. I was blown away. Maleah was soaring above her limitations.

God allowed me to witness another miracle, another blessing and testimony. I was so encouraged. I cried. And I wrote again. This time, I wrote a narrative poem for children about Maleah called "The Busy Baby Bumblebee." It is about a bumblebee that could not see who was treated differently by the bumblebees that could see. In the end, the Busy Baby Bumblebee became the Queen Bee. That was perfect for me because I call all my nieces Princess. But Maleah is the Queen.

Now, do you understand? My story was not for me but for God's glory. It was so I could be there to push and encourage others. **Matthew 5:16** says, "Let your light so shine before men, that they may see your good works, and glorify your Father which is in heaven." All that I have been through has been to glorify God. It was so I could learn to remain strong through it all. It was so I could learn to trust in Jesus and learn to trust in God.

There are more stories I could tell. If I wait another five years, I will have more. But that will be Book Two.

Begin to write your testimony of faith; it may help someone else. What would be the title of your testimony?

CHAPTER 11

SO WHAT?

Whatever? So What? Who cares? Yeah right! Those words used to and at times still cause fire to rage inside of me. Shireyll Moore was the *Whatever* Queen. To think I would write a book called **So(w) What?** in honor of her flippant remarks tickles me. But let me solidify my point with the play on words.

My daughter used to say these things, as if to say she didn't care what was coming next.

Me: "If you do this, that will happen."

Her: "So what."

Me: "You are on punishment."

Her: "Whatever."

It was like she didn't care at all about whatever I would introduce as a consequence to influence her actions or behaviors. Luckily, that was a façade, and she cared, but she was too stubborn to let me know it mattered. There were times I wanted to *spare not* the rod. But she was a smart girl and usually pretty obedient. As I prepared for this message and this book, God told me that for when the enemy was coming after me, I had to develop a *whatever, so what* attitude. God said I could get there, but there were some things I had to practice. I had to learn how to *SOW* some things ahead of time, so I could *REAP* later.

†

The Principles of Sowing and Reaping

Whenever you plant a seed, it doesn't grow or mature overnight. It takes some time. Sometimes it takes watering, but eventually, it will grow. Another principle is whatever you sow, that is what you will reap. You can't sow orange seeds and expect turnips. You can't plant corn and expect tomatoes. What you sow, you shall reap.

Therefore, you can't sow negativity and think you will receive positivity. You can't sow discord and reap harmony. The principle is pretty clear. Just look at Galatians. Here scripture establishes the law or principle.

Galatians 6:

> 7*Do not be deceived: God cannot be mocked. Whatever a man sows, he will*
> *reap in return.* 8*The one who sows to please his flesh, from the flesh will reap destruction; but the one who sows to please the Spirit, from the Spirit will reap eternal life....*

As I recount the stories that I shared in this book, I had to realize that the times I sowed negativity, the times I ate from *The Tree of the Knowledge of Good and Evil*, the times I lost or wavered in my faith, I received all that I had coming. But, God is faithful, and He made a way of escape for me. He gently reminded me who He was and nudged me to know He was there for me. Then, I began to sow good seeds in good ground. I stopped leaning on my own understanding. I began to acknowledge Him in all my ways. I began to let Him direct my paths.

The more I sowed positivity, the better the outcome. The more I saw the glass half full, the more the glass filled up to overflow. Yes, I know it looks crazy right now. I know you sometimes just want to give up. But your breakthrough is about to *burst through*. Focus on Jesus, as Peter did when Jesus allowed him to walk on water. Don't focus on the trial, tribulation, trouble, or tricks. Focus on your outcome, your opportunities, your other side, and overcome.

The Bible says, if you just have faith the size of a grain of a mustard seed.... A mustard seed grows wild and spreads far. Although it is the smallest seed, it grows the biggest plant.

So, what are you sowing? Are you sowing seeds of faith? Are you sowing seeds of unbelief? Think about it. Right now, think about it.

†

I want to be able to face my issues with a Shireyll Moore attitude. So what, devil! Whatever! My

Savior and I got this. *Oh, did you think I would face this problem on my own?* I have learned to eat from the *Tree of Life*. I have learned that *faith with works* is alive. I have learned that no weapon formed against me will prosper. I have learned I can do all things through Christ that strengthens me. I have learned my God is faithful and will make a way of escape for me. I have learned that I am the called, and all things will work out for my good. I have learned to cast my cares upon Him because He cares for me. I have learned that I will win, and the devil will lose. Yes, I have learned! And yet, there is so much more I have yet to learn. And thus, it is time to start all over again with my next journey.

Describe the difference between "SO WHAT" and "SOW WHAT" in your life?

CHAPTER 12

THE PERFECT ENDING TO A NEW BEGINNING

Somewhat like Job, God allowed me to go through my experiences. Sometimes I did right, and sometimes I failed. It was tough. When I failed the test, I knew it right away. But very similar to Job, after all of my trials, God eventually let Satan touch my body. In May of 2017, I was diagnosed with Systemic Lupus. I've heard this is usually hereditary, but as with my son Lowesie, I could not find it anywhere in my blood family.

As I shared earlier, my first response is to look up the signs and symptoms. Two blood tests confirmed the results, and my doctor referred me to a Rheumatologist. Of course, they gave me some suggestions but said that until it worsens, I have to keep moving on. *What? Until it gets worse?*

I have no intention of letting this thing control me. Not at all. I will fight it with everything in me. Me and Jesus. So, as much as people see this diagnosis as a death sentence because they say there is no known cure, I see it as a new beginning. This is my opportunity to put my faith where my heart is... Where my mouth is.

After he lost everything, Job was stricken with boils all over his body. He was in a great deal of pain. However, his friends didn't come to help or comfort him. I am not in that situation. I am experiencing my own battles. I am getting my second spiritual wind. God is increasing my divine assignments, allowing me to share His message, and spread His good news in places I have never been. He allows me to witness His miracles and brand-new mercies day by day.

My Parents

Dede, Calvin, and Me

He has allowed me to see my sister become a Minister, a mother of three, and grandmother of three. The same sister whose life God saved many years ago. That same one whose miracle of life caused me to get saved. He has allowed me to see my big brother get healed from an autoimmune disease and become the father of two boys and grandfather of two girls. He has allowed me to have the best family in the world, beginning with my parents, Lloyd and Shirley Wallace. They left such a powerful legacy. My dad was a man who gave all he had to young people. He wanted to see young people become educated and excel. My mom was a social worker. Her best friend, Norma Dean Totah, encouraged her to enter the field. My mom made a mark in this world. They gave me the best siblings ever, Calvin and Dede. My grandmother called my siblings and first cousins 'the army,' because we fought so much as kids. But our bond is unbreakable, and our love is limitless.

Me and My King....

Words can't describe my husband. He is amazing in so many ways. My next book will be about our amazing 39+ years of a love affair. He is a man of God, a great husband, and an awesome father. He gave me four of the most amazing kids; you have met them in this book.

Michelle is the leader of our family. She is intelligent, beautiful, driven, organized, and compassionate. She is an elementary school principal and has been saved since she was five years old. She has a beautiful voice and gives it all back to God. She married her soulmate, Dakarai Maynard, in July 2019, and they now have two children.

Shireyll is the Assistant Woman's Basketball Coach at Stonybrook University. She looks like me and has taken on much of what I did growing up and then some. She is smart, beautiful, driven, organized, and quietly sensitive. After my mom died, Shireyll began calling me in the morning, because she knew I spoke with my mom daily.

I played basketball at Mount Vernon High School and wore the #12 jersey, as did Shireyll (and two of my nieces). I played college basketball at Fairfield University in Connecticut and wore the #12 jersey, as did Shireyll. I was a member of the National Honor Society, so were Michelle and Shireyll. I was President of the National Honor Society. Shireyll was President of the whole school. She and her husband, Steve, expect their first child in May 2023. Can you tell how proud I am of my girls?

Lowes, III is now a college graduate and is an actor. He is smart, handsome, driven, organized, and passionate. His biggest role was the understudy and stand in for Denzel Washington in *Fences*. One day his break will come, according to God's way.

Isaiah is a college student who is smart, handsome, driven, compassionate, and passionate. He coaches basketball to able-bodied kids. He gives the best hugs ever.

The Fam… with Omar

The Fam… with Nan

My family December 2021

Front Row: Amaya, Joy and Jade, Me, Michelle and Hartley, Shireyll.
The Back Row: Isaiah, Lowes III, Jamayal, Lowes Jr., Dakarai, Dakotah, and Steve.

In 2012, our godson Jamayal moved in with us. His parents passed away when he was a young boy. Today, he is our adopted son, embraced as our own. He and his wife, Joi, have given us our first and third granddaughters, Amaya and Jade.

We also were instrumental in the life of a young man named Omar Ford, who my children identify as their big brother. Omar and his love LaQuita have four children today—Tamir (who has a baby girl), Omarion, Omadia, and Omar.

I am blessed with an awesome family of aunts, uncles, and cousins, who keep me energized and always got my back. I lost my great-aunt, Sweet, in December 2020 due to COVID, my dad's baby sister, Elaine, in September 2022, and my mom's baby brother, Sonny, in October 2022. These losses impacted me greatly, but my love and memories are mine forever. I will continue to make memories with my remaining aunties and uncle.

I have a great relationship with my mother-in-love who supports everything I do. I also married into a family that gave me pretty wonderful aunts, brothers, sisters, nieces, nephews, and cousins.

And I have a slew of godchildren beginning with Jamayal, who is the oldest, followed by DJ, Temarra, Danielle, Mychal, Travis, Tristan, and Mikey.

I have been blessed to be part of the following churches in my lifetime: Church of Our Savior in Yonkers, NY; Mount Vernon Heights Congregational Church, Mount Vernon, NY; Macedonia Baptist Church, Mount Vernon, NY;

Star of Bethlehem Missionary Baptist Church, Albany, NY; Redemption Church of Christ, Troy, NY; and my current church Emmanuel Pentecostal Faith Temple, Mount Vernon, NY. I remain friends with people from each of these churches except the first one because I was too young to remember anyone from there. I really want to honor my spiritual father, the Late Bishop Leon, and Elder Mother Dorothy Dixon, for believing in me. I acknowledge my pastor, Derrick Adams, and his wife, Lade Mel, my ministry team, and Bible class. My church is family to me. God is not through with me yet....

I am grateful to my job and for my team.... They keep me grounded and remind me that the job I do on a daily basis is not just work, but a ministry. I will keep on serving in this capacity until the Lord shifts me.

I pray that this journey you've taken with me has been rewarding and that there were some nuggets of knowledge that you have gleaned. Keep me in prayer, as I embark on a new beginning, sharing my stories and poems as they come, for I will continue to praise my Savior all day long.

Oh, and let me not forget that my last blood test showed no signs of Lupus. SOW WHAT!!!

So, this is not the end but a New Beginning....

Thank you for reading my story. Please share it or parts of it to help someone else. And please leave a positive Review of this book on Amazon by visiting www.tinyurl.com/ReviewSowWhatBook.

ABOUT THE AUTHOR

Patrice Wallace-Moore is a native of both Yonkers and Mount Vernon, NY, as she was born in Yonkers and educated in both Yonkers and Mount Vernon School Districts.

She graduated from Fairfield University and the State University of NY at Albany. She is a New York State licensed Clinical Social Worker who has worked in addiction and mental health for over 30 years. Early in her career, she worked primarily with Adolescents and was a sought-after presenter on Adolescent issues for many years. In 1998, she became a Clinical Director at a drug and alcohol treatment facility in Putnam County, NY, and in 2000, she became the CEO.

Patrice was a member of the New York State Governor's Heroin Task Force. She was also the Co-chair of the New York State Governor's Behavioral Health Service Advisory Council (BHSAC) from 2013-2021. She was also the Chair of the BHSAC Regulations Subcommittee.

Patrice was the head Varsity Basketball Coach at her alma mater, Mount Vernon HS, from 2000-2013. During this time, over twenty players went on to play college basketball. She retired as the winningest basketball coach for the team. In 2016, following the tragic shooting of a 13-year-old aspiring basketball player named Shamoya McKenzie, Patrice, along with her sister and several friends, became owners of the Mt. Vernon Shamrocks Women's Professional Basketball Team of the Women's American Basketball Association (WABA). The team is named after Shamoya, as Shamrock was one of her nicknames.

In 2003, Patrice was ordained as an Elder at the Emmanuel Pentecostal Faith Temple in Mt. Vernon, NY, under the leadership of Bishop Leon and Elder Dr. Dorothy Dixon. Her Pastor today is Elder Derrick Adams, and his First Lady is Melanie Adams.

Patrice married her husband, former NBA Player Elder Lowes Moore, Jr., in 1983. Their marriage has been an inspiring example to so many others. They have four children Michelle (married to Dakarai Maynard), Shireyll (married to Stephen Pogue), Lowes III, and Isaiah. Patrice and Lowes also claim two bonus sons, Omar (married to Laquita) and Jamayal (married to Joi).

Lowes and Patrice now have several grandchildren. Two, Amaya and Jade, are from Jamayal and Joi. Michelle and Dakarai are the parents of Dakotah and Hartley. Steve and Shireyll expect Lanie in May of 2023. Omar and Laquita have four children and one granddaughter.

Patrice's parents, Lloyd and Shirley Wallace, have journeyed beyond their earthly tabernacles awaiting that 'great getting up morning.' But their memories and life teachings continue to guide her, her siblings, Calvin and Dede, and the

Boobaloos (nickname her father gave to his grandchildren).

Readers can contact Patrice Wallace-Moore by email at moorejoy63@gmail.com **or connect with her on Instagram @ceoachp.**

Made in the USA
Middletown, DE
21 August 2023

36872095R00092